OJRIL-
the completely in-com-plete graham chapman

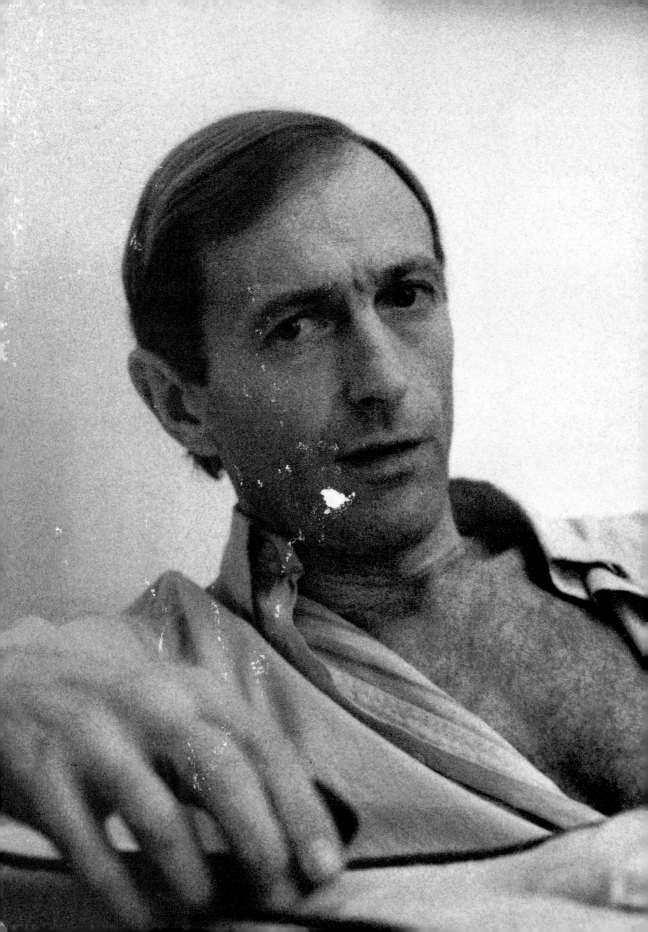

OJRIL- the completely in- com- plete graham chapman

Graham Chapman

Edited by Jim Yoakum

Unpublished scripts from
Monty Python's pipe-smoking
genius

~~Four words~~ Foreword by Eric Idle

Brassey's • Washington, D.C.

Editor's notes

Each script published here is as close as possible to the original.
They have been edited only for spelling and obvious grammatical errors.

Our Show For Ringo Starr was co-written by Douglas Adams and Graham
Chapman partially based on ideas previously developed by Douglas Adams.
The 'B Ark' sequence originally formed the basis of a storyline which Douglas
Adams submitted to the Dr Who programme. He subsequently re-used the sequence
again as part of an episode of The Hitchhiker's Guide to the Galaxy.

The right of the Douglas Adams to be identified as the co-author of 'Our Show for
Ringo Starr' and the author of the 'B Ark' has been asserted by him in accordance
with the Copyright, Designs and Patents Act, 1998.

ISBN 1-57488-270-8

British Library Cataloguing-in-Publication Data.
A catalogue record for this book is available from the British Library.

Designed by Simon Rosenheim
and printed in Spain by Bookprint, S.L, Barcelona

Brassey's
22841 Quicksilver Drive
Dulles, Virginia 20166

First U.S. edition

10 9 8 7 6 5 4 3 2 1

Contents

Foreword

Planet Graham

I recently got back from Mexico. It was the first time I'd been there in 16 years, since filming *Yellowbeard*. So I have been thinking of Graham quite a bit.

Graham was a very strange planet. Since he was drunk so much of the time, he wasn't always the most accurate observer of people. In fact, he was desperately paranoid (probably about his gayness among all those tweedy doctory types), so that's why he got so paralytic. Since he never said much and wrote even less, it was never easy to know just exactly what he was thinking.

Whenever I read some of his work, I notice what a weird view he had of things. He was a wonderful chap.

Eric Idle
January 1998

OUR SHOW FOR RINGO STARR

Involving a Beatle, a Python and the soon-to-be-famous Douglas Adams, *Our Show For Ringo Starr* is perhaps one of the most infamous comedy scripts never produced. Graham said, "I co-wrote this with Douglas Adams and it has Michael Palin to thank for its origin." Well, sort of. Michael Palin is responsible for the creation of a character used in the *Monty Python* television series who was dubbed the 'It's Man'[1] and the It's Man is behind the creation of *Our Show For Ringo Starr*.

Graham explained, "One day we decided to give the It's Man an opportunity to do more, finally to speak his piece, so at the end of show #28 we had Michael, dressed as the It's Man, come out on stage. The idea was that it was to be his show, a chat show, and that he was finally going to be allowed to get the rest of this important sentence out, which had always been interrupted. Guests for this pretend chat show were going to include any famous people we could get.[2] As luck would have it,

[1] The 'It's Man' was a shabbily dressed, hermit-like man who usually struggled across difficult terrain in order to get his sentence out on television. Unfortunately, he could never get beyond the word "It's..." before being interrupted by the opening titles.

[2] John and Yoko were first approached about being the guests on the show. John, a big Monty Python fan, happily agreed, but he and Yoko were involved in an car accident soon after.

Ringo and Lulu obliged to come along to the studio and 'not be interviewed'." Graham and John Cleese had first met Ringo in late 1969, while they were writing and acting in his film, *The Magic Christian* (which also starred Peter Sellers). Ringo's appearance on *Python* not only sparked the idea for *Our Show For Ringo Starr*, but also cemented a lifelong friendship between Ringo and Graham. Graham said, "This gave us the idea to maybe try to work with Ringo again later on, and so a few years later, Douglas Adams and myself wrote a special for Ringo, a part science-fiction, part historical-fiction story that loosely revolved around a few of Ringo's hit songs." Conceived by Graham and Douglas as an hour-long special for American TV, *Our Show For Ringo Starr* was actually a sort of extended promotional film for Ringo's then-current album, *Goodnight Vienna* and was to feature many songs from the LP. It is full of classic Python-style absurdity and the sort of comedic sci-fi lunacy that would later become a hallmark of Douglas' *Hitchhiker's Guide To The Galaxy* novels. In fact, Douglas salvaged one of his ideas from the script, the Golgafrincham B-Ark sequence, and used it in his novel, *The Restaurant At The End of the Universe*.

Said Graham of the script in the late 1980s, "The script was never approved by any networks, or by cable-TV because I think that they thought it a bit rude and because, quite frankly, I don't think they understood it very much. It would have made a very nice show. I highly doubt that it will ever be made now." This script, often rumoured and never fully published before now, was never filmed.

OUR SHOW FOR RINGO STARR

A.K.A. Goodnight Vienna

By Nemona Lethbridge and Vera Hunt
(a.k.a. Graham Chapman and Douglas Adams)

© 1975 Graham Chapman and Douglas Adams
and later, © 1987 Seagoat Productions, Ltd.
except The 'B Ark' © 1974 Douglas Adams.

FIFTEEN TO THIRTY SECONDS OPENING CREDITS.

"I'M THE GREATEST"

RINGO in 'Goodnight Vienna' costume, neutral setting, pointing, like God, at things as we see them happen, including: a rocket launching, an atom bomb exploding, the summit of Everest, a Spanish hotel being blown up and down (FILM and REVERSE FILM) with accompanying ACCORDION MUSIC, New York being flattened by an enormous mouse dropping on it, a knockout punch from Mohammed Ali, Chairman Mao, enormous crowds cheering wildly, paramilitary police shooting up a bed of roses, a person in an ant costume having a cup of tea, he is messily crushed by an enormous boot to cod FAIRY-TALE MUSIC.

Throughout the following we see SHOTS of typical happy fairy-tale-type rustic villages, princes, knights, Little Bo Beeps, Dragons, etc... During the narration all the characters become aware that the narration isn't talking about them and stand looking at the camera bemused that their stories are not being taken up.

> NARRATOR
> [V.O.]
> Once upon a time, a long time ago; ooh,
> it must have been, ooh, ages — so long
> ago, I can't remember it, and my friend
> Godfrey, who's 37, he can't remember
> it, so it must have been a long time
> ago. I mean come on, I'm not talking
> about measly little bits of time,
> minutes and all that, but proper grown-
> up years and I mean lots of them.
> Anyway, a long time ago in a far, far
> land, I mean a really long way, I mean
> you may think it's a long way down the
> road to the hardware store, but that's
> just peanuts to this sort of distance,
> there lived a handsome prince. Well,
> not particularly handsome in fact,
> though bits of him were handsome, I
> mean where do you draw the line? I mean
> some people find long flowing blonde

hair and a retroussé nose very
handsome. I mean, I don't personally,
but then all opinions are subjective.
If I had to, I'd say that I prefer the
sort who's dark, stocky and good at
maths.

We see the following happening as the narrator speaks.

> NARRATOR
> [V.O.]
> Anyway, this prince, whom some people
> probably found attractive, was out
> walking in the woods one day, when he
> fell off a cliff and died very messily,
> which prevented him from living happily
> ever after.

Stunned shock look on the faces of all the characters.

> NARRATOR
> [V.O.]
> But his great, great, great, great,
> great grandson worked in an office.

CUT TO: OFFICE

> FAIRY-TALE CHARACTERS
> [V.O.]
> What? What about us?

> DIRECTOR
> [V.O.]
> Sorry loves, that's all.

> FAIRY-TALE CHARACTERS
> [V.O.]
> What? It took me hours to get into this
> costume.

> DIRECTOR
> [V.O.]
> Well, that's all there is.

                    FAIRY-TALE CHARACTERS
                           [V.O.]
          Look can't we be in one more shot?

                          DIRECTOR
                           [V.O.]
          Alright, alright.

3-SECOND SHOT of fairy-tale characters waving at the camera
then CUT BACK TO: OFFICE.

                    FAIRY-TALE CHARACTERS
                           [V.O.]
          Well that wasn't much better — do we
          still get the whole fee?

In office RINGO is standing leaning against the desk.

                          RINGO
          Have you done now — can we get on with
          it?

                          NARRATOR
                           [V.O.]
          Well...

CAMERA BEGINS TO PULL AWAY.

                          NARRATOR
                           [V.O.]
          Ah yes.

CAMERA JUMPS BACK.

                          RINGO
          Well I'm glad to hear that I've been
          hanging around here for hours.

                          NARRATOR
                           [V.O.]
          Anyway this person who was extremely boring
          and uninteresting worked in this dull drab
          office, it's impossible to say how
          appallingly dull and boring it all was.

                    RINGO
Look, just leave it to me will you.

                  NARRATOR
                  [V.O.]
What!

                    RINGO
Push off!

                  NARRATOR
                  [V.O.]
Well, I haven't finished yet.

                    RINGO
Yes, you have, you are not needed.

                  NARRATOR
                  [V.O.]
Do I still get a full fee?

                    RINGO
Shut up. Now at last I can get on with
it.

RINGO stands against the wall and holds two handles. The
wall section PIVOTS BACKWARDS like Thunderbirds and Ringo
goes down a chute

                    RINGO
                (muttering)
Bloody narrators.

                  NARRATOR
                  [V.O.]
I heard that.

                    RINGO
Good!

The first few bars of the PIANO INTRO to 'ALL BY MYSELF'
while RINGO slides down a chute. An automatic device gives
him sticks and costumes on the way down, another device puts
a custard pie in his face, another wipes it off. He drops

out onto a drum stool with the Band just as the drum part
starts.

First verse: SHOT of back drop of curtains, CLOSE-UP of band
etc...

Second verse: CSO CLOSE-UP of RINGO. PULL BACK to reveal he
is in an open car going to New York. SHOTS highlight non-
communication, loneliness, etc...

END OF SONG: THUNDERBIRDS FILM REVERSED.

RINGO is now back in his office.

JAMES McTOOTHBUCKET arrives, dressed like a very rich
businessman. He is riding piggy-back on a uniformed black
CHAUFFEUR who's wearing a chauffeur's uniform.

The CHAUFFEUR steps out from under McTOOTHBUCKET, who is
actually suspended from wires which we don't see. CHAUFFEUR
is still holding one hand under McTOOTHBUCKET's foot. He
then puts out his other hand lower [REPEAT] for
McTOOTHBUCKET to step on, to take McTOOTHBUCKET to ground
level as if he is climbing down steps to a carriage. Just
before McTOOTHBUCKET reaches ground, the CHAUFFEUR unrolls
with his free hand a red carpet which takes him up to
RINGO's desk.

RINGO goes up to the CHAUFFEUR now standing to attention,
takes out a duster, spits on it and polishes the CHAUFFEUR's
spectacles, gives a quick rub to the CHAUFFEUR's body, takes
a pen out of the CHAUFFEUR's inside pocket, wipes it down
with an oily rag, puts it back, takes it out again, looks at
it, nods, puts it back again. He takes a petrol hose from
the side of the filing cabinet filed under 'G' and puts it
down the back of the CHAUFFEUR's trousers.

> RINGO
> (aside to camera)
> And this is only Tuesday.

The CHAUFFEUR glides off without moving his legs. RINGO puts
hose back in filing cabinet under 'G', does a double-take
and picks out a rabbit.

> RINGO
> Oh, that shouldn't be in there. Ah,
> rabbit, rabbit, rabbit.

RINGO puts rabbit in filing cabinet under 'R'. McTOOTHBUCKET
starts to sit down, RINGO puts a chair under him.
McTOOTHBUCKET holds out one hand, RINGO puts a cigar in it.
McTOOTHBUCKET holds out his other hand, RINGO puts a lighter
in it. McTOOTHBUCKET lights his own cigar. RINGO takes the
lighter from him. McTOOTHBUCKET slightly changes the shape
of his hand. RINGO responds, puts a brandy glass in it.
McTOOTHBUCKET tosses back the brandy, RINGO takes the glass
from him. McTOOTHBUCKET holds out his right arm in a curve,
holds out his left hand and does rapid pronation and
supination. RINGO looks bemused and then the light dawns.
RINGO goes to the cupboard and picks out a GIRL, puts her on
McTOOTHBUCKET's lap so that she sits in the crook of his
right arm, with her right tit automatically fondled by his
left hand. McTOOTHBUCKET moves his left hand with his finger
pointed downwards. RINGO pushes the intercom under his
finger so that the finger hits the right button.

                    McTOOTHBUCKET
          Next.

RINGO picks the GIRL off McTOOTHBUCKET's lap and sends her
down the chute. He then turns to the cupboard and closes it,
but we see GIRL #2 in it waiting for similar treatment
tomorrow.

                       RINGO
          I don't have to do this job you know.

He goes over to McTOOTHBUCKET, sprays deodorant under his
arms, then in the telephone, then in McTOOTHBUCKET's mouth.

                       RINGO
          I could have been an ashtray.

RINGO exits backwards, bowing.
CUT TO: RINGO walking down the corridor. We see more
chauffeur-driven walking. A CLOSE-UP on RINGO'S face, very
dramatic.

                       RINGO
          I think I'll have some coffee.

NARRATOR
[V.O.]
And after that typically boring remark
about coffee, which can't have
interested anybody...

RINGO
It's you again. I thought I told you to
push off.

NARRATOR
[V.O.]
Our hero's life suddenly became very
interesting.

RINGO
What!

NARRATOR
[V.O.]
Oh, nothing, nothing. I'm going.

RINGO
What was that about my life becoming
interesting?

NARRATOR
[V.O.]
It's alright, I know when I'm not
wanted.

RINGO
Look, how does my life become
interesting?

NARRATOR
[V.O.]
Well, I was going to explain how you
became amazingly rich and popular and
had as many birds as you wanted with
really enormous knockers, but you made
it clear to me that I'm not wanted, so
I'm off.

                         RINGO
Look! Stop here a moment, will you?

                         NARRATOR
                         [V.O.]
Alright.

Pause.

                         RINGO
Now look...

                         NARRATOR
                         [V.O.]
Double my fee.

                         RINGO
What!

                         NARRATOR
                         [V.O.]
I said double my fee.

                         RINGO
Alright, but no more going on about how
boring I am.

                         NARRATOR
                         [V.O.]
Well, alright... Just a little bit?

                         RINGO
No!

                         NARRATOR
                         [V.O.]
Alright, alright.

                         RINGO
Well, what happens?

                         NARRATOR
                         [V.O.]
Look out of the window.

RINGO looks out of the window. MIX INTO: EXISTING FILM of 'ONLY YOU'. During this song, BRIEF CUT-AWAY TO: RINGO in corridor.

> RINGO
>
> Is that me?

> NARRATOR
> [V.O.]
>
> No.

> RINGO
>
> Oh, come on.

> NARRATOR
> [V.O.]
>
> Wait, can't you?

MIX BACK TO: SONG
SONG ENDS.
CUT BACK TO: CORRIDOR.

> RINGO
>
> Well, that was nice, but what's it got to do with me?

> NARRATOR
> [V.O.]
>
> Wait, will you...

GIRL #3 with large breasts seen approaching.

> RINGO
>
> Is this one of mine?

> NARRATOR
> [V.O.]
>
> No.

> RINGO
>
> Look, I'm beginning to have second thoughts about that fee.

GIRL #3 looks at him curiously because he seems to be talking to himself.

                    GIRL #3
          What are you doing?

                    RINGO
          I'm talking to my narrator.

                    GIRL #3
          Your narrator?

                    RINGO
          Yes, haven't you got one?

GIRL #3 screams.

                    GIRL #3
               Look!

The wall behind them is seen to be disintegrating.

                    RINGO
               What? Oh that. It's just my life
               becoming more interesting.

GIRL #3 runs off.

                    RINGO
               Strange girl.

Through a hole we see an enormous metallic foot, which then
shrinks and we see it belongs to a silver ROBOT, like the
one on the 'Goodnight Vienna' cover. ROBOT walks through the
wall, atomising the GIRL #3 as she runs off.

                    RINGO
               Oh well, I didn't like her anyway. Good
               afternoon.

                    ROBOT
          Are you Rinog Trars?

                    RINGO
          No, but it's close.

                         ROBOT
          Rinog Trars, I have been sent by our
          masters in the galaxy of Smegmon to
          pass on to you the ancestral powers of
          your race, the Jenkinsons.

                         RINGO
          I think you've got the wrong bloke.

                         ROBOT
          My circuits are infallible, there can
          be no error.

                         RINGO
          But I'm not Rinog Trars.

                         ROBOT
          Error, impossible, error impossible.

                         RINGO
          My name's Ringo Starr.

                         ROBOT
          That's what I said.

                         RINGO
          No it isn't.

                         ROBOT
          Shut up. It's near enough, I've had a
          hard day. Come with me!

                         RINGO
          I can't. I'm not free till five.

                         ROBOT
          I will free you.

                         RINGO
          Well, you'd better see the boss.

     ROBOT looks at his watch.

                        ROBOT
    Oh, alright.

CUT TO: BOSS'S OFFICE. We see ROBOT standing in front of
BOSS's desk. Behind ROBOT is a series of ROBOT-shaped holes
in the walls of other offices he has walked through, the
edges of which are still smoking. He has obviously passed
through several offices on the way. We also see RINGO, a few
walls behind, climbing through the holes. Several puzzled
faces appear at the holes. We hear conversation between the
nearest pair of heads.

                        WOMAN
    What on earth was that?

                        MAN
    Must be the telephone sanitisers.

                        WOMAN
    Oh, I'd forgotten it was Tuesday.

CUT TO: BOSS
                        BOSS
    I'm sorry I can't see anyone without an
    appointment.

                        ROBOT
    Oh dear. How soon can you fit me in?

                        BOSS
                    (into intercom)
    Miss Lewis, how many have we got
    outside?

                        MISS LEWIS
    Oh about twelve, Mr Maelstrom.

                        BOSS
    Well that'll be two or three days.

                        RINGO
    Couldn't you fit him in first? He only
    wants a quick word.

> BOSS
>
> Mr Starkey, we paid a team of
> management consultants a very large sum
> of money to devise this system of
> appointments, so you are surely not
> suggesting that I cast banknotes to the
> wind in these times of monstrous and
> swinging economic stress by jacking it?

> RINGO
>
> Does that mean no?

> BOSS
>
> Affirmative.

> RINGO
>
> Does that mean yes?

> BOSS
>
> I think so.

> RINGO
>
> Oh dear. (To ROBOT) Can you come back
> next week?

ROBOT's visor opens up. A piercing beam of light
disintegrates the wall with door in it, revealing a waiting
room full of people. He disintegrates them all, leaving just
a charred secretary sitting at a smouldering desk.

> BOSS
>
> Oh, well it would appear that I do have
> a moment, so what would seem to be the
> problem?

> ROBOT
>
> This man must come with me. He will
> inherit great powers.

> BOSS
>
> Oh well, not in working hours I'm
> afraid. You see, he's not free till
> five.

                         ROBOT
          Now!

                         BOSS
          No, I'm afraid not. That has to be my
          last word.

                         ROBOT
          If you will free this man, I will give
          you the whole world.

                         BOSS
          Mmmm, tempting. But on balance I think
          probably not. I mean, it's in a little
          bit of a financial mess at the moment.
          I don't want to find myself sitting up
          half the night sorting out the parity
          of the Yen, or the whole weekend
          sifting through the socio-economic
          problems of the Indian sub-continent,
          or miss my Sunday afternoon's golfing
          by averting war in the Middle East. I
          mean, that's not what I'd call a
          bargain.

                         ROBOT
          Well what would you like to have then?

                         BOSS
          Canada?

                         ROBOT
          And so you shall!

SOUND OF 'TING!'. CSO SHOT of BOSS standing outside the
Government buildings of Ottawa.

                         BOSS
          Oh thank you very much.

He turns and walks towards the buildings.
CUT BACK TO: OFFICE. RINGO and ROBOT but no BOSS

                         RINGO
          Right. Can I have my powers please?

                         ROBOT
          We must be somewhere private.

They move out to the corridor.

                         RINGO
          There isn't anywhere. There's only this
          john.

                         ROBOT
          The john?

                         RINGO
          Yeah, the john. The bog, the comfort
          station, the thunderbox, little boy's
          room.

                         ROBOT
          Ah! The lavatory.

                         RINGO
          Something like that, yes.

                         ROBOT
          Won't people talk?

                         RINGO
          Let them. I don't care. There's no law
          about being in the lavatory with a
          robot.

They are entering the lavatory.
CUT TO: SENATOR #1 talking to Senate.

                       SENATOR #1
          ...This depraved and corrupt practice
          must be stamped out!

A laser beam atomises him.
CUT BACK TO: RINGO and ROBOT in urinals.
ROBOT's visor is going down.

                    RINGO
        Show off.

                    ROBOT
        Are we alone?

                    RINGO
        Hang on... (shouting) Money!!

Looks at closed doors.

                    RINGO
        We're alone.

                    ROBOT
        And so the powers...

He holds up his arms. There is a flash of light.

                    RINGO
        Is that it?

                    ROBOT
        Yes.

                    RINGO
        Why all the privacy?

ROBOT goes red.

                    ROBOT
        I'm easily embarrassed.

                    RINGO
        Are you sure you've given me the
        powers?

                    ROBOT
        Yes.

                    RINGO
        They're a bit dull, aren't they?

                        NARRATOR
                         [V.O.]
             And so it was that he was given dull
             powers, powers so ineffably dull that
             by comparison...

                         RINGO
             Can you do anything about narrators?

ROBOT's visor drops, a laser beam shoots out.

                        NARRATOR
                         [V.O.]
             ...Dullness itself — aghhhhh!

                         ROBOT
             You are now free to travel through time
             and space at will.

CUT TO: RINGO in Roman arena with lion charging at him.
CUT BACK TO: RINGO and ROBOT in urinals.

                         RINGO
             He's right. Anything else?

                         ROBOT
             What?

                         RINGO
             Any other powers?

                         ROBOT
             Yes, you can go into nightclubs.

                         RINGO
             Good!

                         ROBOT
             You can write television situation comedy.

                         RINGO
                      (doubtfully)
             Hmmmmmmmm...

                    ROBOT
          And you can do quite nice flower
          arrangements.

                    RINGO
          That'll be useful.

                    ROBOT
          And merely by doing this (he waves a
          hand), you can destroy the entire
          universe.

                    RINGO
          What, just that?

He starts to wave his hand. The screen shakes. We hear a
RUMBLE. ROBOT clamps RINGO's hand, but still the lavatory
doors fall off. We see a MAN #2 wearing a deaf-aid hurriedly
pulling up his trousers.

                    MAN #2
          Hey!

He goes back into the cubical.

                    RINGO
          Well what do I do now?

                    ROBOT
          You must cast out your past life.

                    RINGO
          How do I do that?

                    ROBOT
          Sing it.

                    RINGO
          If that's supposed to be a link into a
          song, I can do better myself.

He goes into the lavatory, sits on it, flushes it. It
revolves and becomes his seat at the drums with the Band
around him. INTO SONG 'SNOOKEROO'.

First verse: CLOSE-UP SHOTS of Band, then with CSO
BACKGROUND SHOTS of Liverpool, Birmingham, Huton etc...
SEPIA STILLS, GREEN STILLS, TINTED PHOTOGRAPHS, BLACK AND
WHITE PHOTOGRAPHS BADLY TINTED INTO COLOUR. END OF SONG.

CUT TO: CLOSE-UP of ROBOT'S face. When we PULL BACK, we see
that ROBOT and RINGO are drifting through space with a star
background. We hear ELECTRONIC HUM — ELECTRONIC MUSIC. RINGO
is now wearing a glittering super-hero costume.

> ROBOT
>> Time is an illusion, it's merely a
>> moving point of focus.

> RINGO
>> That's nice.

> ROBOT
>> The concept of a four-dimensional
>> space—time continuum inevitably leads to
>> the entelechy of space—time
>> transportation in the doughnut of the
>> universe.

> RINGO
>> The concept of a four-dimensional
>> space—time continuum inevitably suggests
>> the universe looks like a prawn
>> omelette.

> ROBOT
>> Who said that?

> RINGO
>> Don't know, must have been me. I felt
>> my lips move.

CUT TO: MORE DISTANCE SHOTS of RINGO and ROBOT against a
star background. We see a planet with a line of moons
extending from it, with a slab between them, like the shot
in '2001: A Space Odyssey'.
We see RINGO and ROBOT drifting towards it, SWING ROUND to
reveal that it is in fact a battered old door. ROBOT opens
the door. Through the door frame we see an ordinary customs

hall. RINGO has a quick walk around the door frame, we don't
see him on the other side. Then he follows the ROBOT in
through the door.
CUT TO: INSIDE. We see them entering with the star
background seen through the door. There is a spaceship
passing by.
The CUSTOMS OFFICER is totally normal, except that he has
green skin and a little blue moustache.

> CUSTOMS OFFICER
> Anything to declare?

> RINGO
> What do you mean? I'm travelling
> through time.

> CUSTOMS OFFICER
> And where have you come from?

> RINGO
> Mid-1970s.

> CUSTOMS OFFICER
> Could you be more specific?

> RINGO
> No. We have to think of repeats.

> CUSTOMS OFFICER
> Of course. And where are you going to?

> RINGO
> Ah, Rome.

CUSTOMS OFFICER stamps piece of paper and gives it to him.
INSTANT CUT-AWAY TO: RINGO standing in obviously modern Rome
CSO. He turns his eyes heavenward.
CUT BACK TO: CUSTOMS HALL

> RINGO
> No, _ancient_ Rome.

> CUSTOMS OFFICER
> I see sir. What year?

                    RINGO
Well, Julius Caesar and all that.

                    CUSTOMS OFFICER
I see sir. About 44 B.C.

                    RINGO
Yes, that'll do.

                    CUSTOMS OFFICER
Got any cameras, watches, cigarette
lighters, intoxicating spirits, explosive
weaponry, American magazines, heating
appliances, hamburgers, telescopes, zips,
buttons, artificial kidney, penicillin,
Pepsi-Cola, prawn omelettes, Anglepoise
lamps, T-shirts, griddle cakes, barbecue
sauce, laudromats -

                    RINGO
No!

                    CUSTOMS OFFICER
Good.

                    RINGO
Why?

                    CUSTOMS OFFICER
Because they hadn't been invented then.

                    RINGO
Oh, I hadn't thought of that.

                    CUSTOMS OFFICER
That's what we're here for sir.

                    RINGO
Well I've got my friend.

He indicates to ROBOT.

                    CUSTOMS OFFICER
Oh, they were very broad-minded then, sir.

At this point a very large alien creature enters. It looks like a very large prawn. It's probably green. It moves its tentacles in rather camp balletic gestures. It knocks RINGO to the ground.

                    PRAWN
          Excuse me honey, but I think I was
          first.

                    RINGO
               (from the ground)
          Oh, go ahead.

                    CUSTOMS OFFICER
          Yes, madam?

                    PRAWN
               (sounding like Bette Davis)
          Don't be cheeky!

The PRAWN slaps the CUSTOMS OFFICER with a tentacle, turns and sees ROBOT.

                    PRAWN
          Now that I like.

ROBOT goes red. PRAWN goes over to ROBOT and the two begin to hit it off very well. RINGO returns to CUSTOMS OFFICER.

                    RINGO
          Can I get off to ancient Rome now please?

                    CUSTOMS OFFICER
          Not yet you can't sir.

                    RINGO
          Why not?

                    CUSTOMS OFFICER
          You haven't filled in the form.

                    RINGO
          What form? I've been given the power to
          travel in time and space.

                    CUSTOMS OFFICER
          Oh, oh, oh... You've been given the
          power to travel in time and space.

He calls to all his mates who crowd around to mock.

                    CUSTOMS OFFICER
          Come over here, he's been given the
          power to travel in time and space. And
          I suppose you're Rinog Trars and can
          destroy the universe just like that!

He waves his hand.

                    RINGO
          Well, no I'm not him.

                    CUSTOMS OFFICER
          I thought not.

                    RINGO
          But I can destroy the universe just
          like that.

                    CUSTOMS OFFICER
          Oh, he can destroy the universe! He
          just thought he would mention in
          passing that he could destroy the
          universe...

He slaps a fish on the counter.

                    CUSTOMS OFFICER
          Fry that fish!

                    RINGO
          What?

                    CUSTOMS OFFICER
          Fry that fish.

                    RINGO
          I can't do that.

> CUSTOMS OFFICER
> Oh, he can destroy the universe but he
> can't fry that fish, can you?

> RINGO
> No.

> CUSTOMS OFFICER
> Well I can.

He digs his finger into the fish, which immediately sizzles.

> CUSTOMS OFFICER
> There, that is a fried fish. A grilled
> brill for the pedantic. Let's see what
> you can do with a haddock, better
> still, there's a gurnet — griddle it.

> RINGO
> I can't do that. But I have got powers.

> CUSTOMS OFFICER
> Oh, powers, powers, powers, eh? I bet
> you couldn't even poach a prawn.

> RINGO
> Well, I can do quite good flower
> arranging.

> CUSTOMS OFFICER
> That's nothing to do with fish.

> RINGO
> Well?

> CUSTOMS OFFICER
> Flower arranging. It's hardly a
> passport to adventure.

> RINGO
> Well neither's fish.

CUSTOMS OFFICER
Listen, you lay off fish. I can do
anything with fish. Now there's a
power, mate.

RINGO
Well what can you do with fish?

CUSTOMS OFFICER
I can braise, fry, deep-fry, heat
through, stew, casserole, simmer or
steam fish with just a single finger.
Any fish, you name it. Alright, carp.
Do you want to know what can be done
with a carp? You come around to my
place and I'll show you what can be
done with a carp.

RINGO
I just want to go through Customs.

CUSTOMS OFFICER
Oh, fish not good enough for you. You
don't care about them do you?

RINGO
Yes I do.

CUSTOMS OFFICER
No you don't.

RINGO
I do. I care a lot about fish.

CUSTOMS OFFICER
No you don't. You don't give a damn
about them.

RINGO
Yes I do.

CUSTOMS OFFICER
Don't.

                    RINGO
         Alright, I don't.

                  CUSTOMS OFFICER
         Don't what?

                    RINGO
         Care about fish.

CUSTOMS OFFICER picks up enormous fish and knocks RINGO over
with it.

                  CUSTOMS OFFICER
         Now you do.

SCREEN BEGINS TO DISSOLVE. MIX INTO 'NO NO' SONG.

                   NARRATOR
              [V.O. with reverb on voice]
         And so the narrator, who bore no ill
         feeling despite having been given the
         boot, and having been killed by a robot
         — nevertheless selflessly, bearing no
         grudge, with no trace of resentment at
         the way he's been treated, comes back
         to say that the story has ended.

                    RINGO
                   [V.O.]
         We haven't finished yet.

                   NARRATOR
                   [V.O.]
         And the narrator went on to describe
         how these lovely scantily clad sixteen-
         year-old ladies who were all bronzed,
         lithe and supple, glided towards him on
         the lonely beach, wantonly displaying
         the bit between their belly buttons and
         where the hair starts.

During this we begin to see the most EROTIC and PROVOCATIVE
SHOTS that we can get away with on American television as
described in the speech.

                    NARRATOR
                    [V.O.]
          And so the narrator didn't say anything
          for several days.

                    RINGO
                    [V.O.]
          I think I'll go there instead.

We see women crawling all over the NARRATOR now.

                    NARRATOR
          No, I'm afraid you can't — this is for
          narrators only. It's just one of the
          perks of the job. And then the
          narrator...

                    RINGO
                    [V.O.]
          Look, get on with my story, will you?

                    NARRATOR
          And so our hero decided to go back to
          Ancient Rome, not as an Emperor, but as
          a common peasant...

                    RINGO
                    [V.O.]
          When did I decide that?

CUT TO: RINGO as a Roman peasant in an idyllic setting — a
mossy bank surrounded by olive trees, the odd column and an
idyllic stream with girls bathing.

                    RINGO
          Oh, it's not so bad after all! I think
          I'm going to enjoy this.

A whip lashes across him. CAMERA PULLS BACK to reveal that
the whip is held by an enormous ROMAN SOLDIER #1.

                    ROMAN SOLDIER #1
          Slave! Where is Flavius?

                         RINGO
              Who?

                    ROMAN SOLDIER #1
              That idle friend of yours. Where is he?

                         RINGO
              I haven't got a friend.

ROMAN SOLDIER #1 lashes him again.

                    ROMAN SOLDIER #1
              The person you were with.

                         ŘINGO
              The only person I was with is being
              embarrassed by the attentions of a
              seven-foot prawn.

Lash...

                         RINGO
              It's true! He's about that big and made
              of tin.

Lash...

                         RINGO
              Don't do that or I'll destroy the
              universe.

Lash...

                         RINGO
              I'm getting out of this. I think I'll
              be a soldier.

ROMAN SOLDIER #1 lashes out with his whip again but RINGO
disappears as the whip wraps itself around the soldier.
CUT TO: RINGO dressed as a soldier marching in column.

                         RINGO
              Ah, that's better.

He turns to the soldier next to him.

                RINGO
Have we been marching long?

            ROMAN SOLDIER #2
Since dawn.

                RINGO
Have we got much further to go?

            ROMAN SOLDIER #2
Be careful, you're in enough trouble
already.

                RINGO
Why?

            ROMAN SOLDIER #2
You've been talking all morning.

                RINGO
I have not.

Whip descends on him again.

                RINGO
Look, gerroff — I'm a soldier — you
can't do that to me.

Lash...

                RINGO
      (to soldier next to him)
Is he always like this?

Lash...

                RINGO
Right, I've had enough. I'm going to be
an Emperor.

CUT TO: RINGO as Caesar on a throne. Purple robes, laurel
leaves, bowl of grapes by his side from which he is being

fed. Senators surround his throne. The crowd yells "Hail Mighty Caesar!"

> RINGO
> Oh, this is better.

He looks around to senators standing behind him.

> RINGO
> You haven't got a whip behind there, have you?

> ROMAN SENATOR
> What? Oh, no, no.

> RINGO
> Well I know you've got something there behind your back, haven't you?

> ROMAN SENATOR
> Oh? Oh, oh, this.

He holds out a dagger, rather embarrassed.

> RINGO
> Oh, that's alright then.

BRUTUS kneels in front of him.

> BRUTUS
> I kiss thy hand but not in flattery Caesar, desiring only thee that Publius Cimber may have an immediate freedom of repeal.

> RINGO
> (to ROMAN SENATOR)
> Who's he?

> ROMAN SENATOR
> Brutus.

> RINGO
> Hello Brutus. Are there any nice girls around here?

                    CASSIUS
          Pardon Caesar, Caesar pardon. As low as
          to thy feet does Cassius fall to beg
          enfranchisement for Publius Cimber.

RINGO is eating grapes.

                    RINGO
          Here, have a few grapes...

CASCA holding up his dagger. All immediately draw daggers.

                    CASCA
          Speak hands for me!

                    RINGO
          Bloody hell.

RINGO disappears.

                    BRUTUS
          Where's he gone?

                    CASSIUS
          Greasy bastard.

                    CASCA
          After him lads!

                    BRUTUS
          Shh...

                    BRUTUS
                 (calling out)
          Come on Julius, we didn't mean it, you
          can come out now. We're all... We
          thought we'd just nip out for a drink
          with the lads. You fancy coming along?

He signals to CASSIUS to stand by the door with a big club.

                    BRUTUS
          Honestly, look, we've thrown all our
          knives to the floor.

They haven't in fact. BRUTUS knocks over something very
metallic.
SCENE DISSOLVES.
CUT BACK TO: CUSTOMS HALL. RINGO is seen getting up off the
floor.

> CUSTOMS OFFICER
> Did you enjoy your trip then?

We see him putting the fish away.

> RINGO
> I preferred being hit by that fish.

> CUSTOMS OFFICER
> Fish? Fish? What fish was that sir?

> RINGO
> The fish you just hit me with.

> CUSTOMS OFFICER
> I haven't hit you with a fish.

> RINGO
> Yes you have.

> CUSTOMS OFFICER
> No I haven't sir. I think the time
> travel is confusing you a bit — you're
> thinking of the fish I'm about to hit
> you with.

> RINGO
> Oh. You're probably right.

CUSTOMS OFFICER hits RINGO with a very large fish again.
DISSOLVE INTO SONG 'HUSBANDS AND WIVES'. The back drop to
the song is scenes of gladiators and bull fights. Very
stylised carnage.
END OF SONG
CUT BACK TO: CUSTOMS HALL. RINGO is on the floor again.

> RINGO
> Will you stop hitting me with that fish?

RINGO stands up.

                    CUSTOMS OFFICER
          What fish?

                    RINGO
          The fish you... (pauses for thought)
          were about to hit me with.

                    CUSTOMS OFFICER
          I wasn't about to hit you with a fish,
          I just did.

                    RINGO
              (getting confused and wary)
          Did you?

                    CUSTOMS OFFICER
          Yes, you remember, it was like this.

He swings with the fish again but RINGO stops it with his
hand.

                    RINGO
          Stop that! Have you seen my mate?

                    CUSTOMS OFFICER
          Yes, he's in there.

He indicates a door which RINGO starts to go through.

                    CUSTOMS OFFICER
          I wouldn't go in.

It is too late, RINGO has gone in.
CUT TO: BEDROOM.
RINGO sees ROBOT and PRAWN in bed together. ROBOT goes very red.

                    RINGO
          Look stop that. Let's get out of here,
          I want to go into the future.

                    ROBOT
          Just five more minutes.

                        RINGO
        Oh, alright...

CUT TO: 'SUNSHINE LIFE FOR ME'
END OF SONG
BACK TO BEDROOM SCENE

                        ROBOT
        Alright, I'm ready.

ELECTRONIC HUM. The bodies of RINGO and ROBOT DISSOLVE —
ELECTRONICALLY — we see VERY QUICK SHOTS of them against a
star background — then a SHOT of a starship in space.
CUT TO: RINGO and ROBOT materialising in grotty garage
setting. There are various, very obviously second-hand cars
dotted around. A sign 'Ron's Garage'. A man[3], JACK, comes up
to RINGO.

                        JACK
        Can I help you?

                        RINGO
        Oh, I'm sorry, I thought that I was
        going to the future.

                        JACK
        Oh well, this is it. This is the future
        alright.

                        RINGO
        No, no, I thought that this was a
        starship.

                        JACK
        Starship, yes, this is a starship —
        latest model starship. (He pats car)
        Beautiful body work.

                        RINGO
        No, I, er meant more of a rocket ship
        travelling through galaxies.

[3] In the margin of the original script either Graham or Douglas had scribbled 'Kieth Moon' (sic),
implying that they wanted the Who drummer and Chapman friend, Keith Moon, to play this role.

                    JACK

Oh! We do all that here, intergalactic
travel, resprays, upholstery,
remoulds...

                    RINGO

I think I'll try somewhere else.

                    JACK

No, no — you want a spaceship, you've
come to the right place. Steady as a
rock, this one, you wouldn't believe
that we are now travelling at one
hundred and fifty thousand miles per
second through the Crab Nebula.

                    RINGO

No.

                    JACK

Marvellous suspension.

Enter MECHANIC.

                    MECHANIC

Hey Jack, have you seen that new
carburettor?

                    JACK

Ha, ha, ha.
            (Aside to Mechanic)
We have a customer.
Look, will you go back to work on the
space warp?

                    MECHANIC

What?

                    JACK

Yes, this is a spaceship.

                    MECHANIC

What? Oh! Is that a customer or
something?

                    JACK
        Yes.

                  MECHANIC
        Oh hell. Yes, I'll do that first.

                    JACK
        (To Ringo) Anyway, how about this one,
        sir? (He pats car.) Anyway, very nice —
        last year's model. I can offer it to
        you at the ridiculous price of two
        thousand, or one-five in part exchange
        for your old one.

He points at ROBOT.

                   RINGO
        Look, this is a garage.

                    JACK
        No it isn't, it's a spaceship. Now how
        about this one? Latest model, falls
        apart as soon as you get it. Saves wear
        and tear.

                   RINGO
        I don't want to buy a car. I think we
        had better get going.

JACK dashes into his little glass prefab office and speaks
not very surreptitiously into a public address system.

                    JACK
        Ah! This is the Captain speaking,
        attention please. Would all personnel
        on the starship... The starship 'Ron' —

He holds up a rather crude sign painted 'STARSHIP RON'.

                    JACK
        — Please buy a car immediately.

He leaves the cubicle.

                        JACK
            Ah, so you wanted a car, sir!

                        RINGO
            Come on. let's go. (To ROBOT) You and
            your powers... Fine spaceship this one
            — we had better go and have your
            computer looked at. Is this still under
            guarantee?

They move towards the door.

                        JACK
            Tell you what I'll do just for you,
            sir. As we're on a spaceship, special
            offer latest sports model, drop dead,
            8-track stereo, tripletone paintwork,
            twin exhausts, sundym glass, genuine
            leather-look upholstery, real plastic
            steering wheel...

During this RINGO and ROBOT reach the door. They open it
outwards towards camera so we don't see it. As RINGO and
ROBOT disappear through it, the JACK shouts after them.

                        JACK
            No down payment, nothing to pay over
            three years.

CUT TO: OUTSIDE OF THE DOOR. RINGO and ROBOT find themselves in
a very Kubrickish spaceship interior. RINGO does dramatic
double-take, snatches open door again. Inside it is the garage.

                        MAN
            (Still as if it's a rather badly disguised lie)
            Yes, starship.

RINGO closes door again.

                        RINGO
            We are on a spaceship.

                        ROBOT
            I told you we were.

> RINGO
>
> No you didn't. You didn't at all. You
> haven't said a word since you went off
> with that Prawn.

ROBOT starts to go red again.

> RINGO
>
> Oh, don't get embarrassed again.
> There's no law against going to bed
> with a prawn.

CUT TO: U.S. SENATE AGAIN. Same scene as before — SENATOR #2
standing by a charred skeleton of the previous senator.

> SENATOR #2
>
> ...and to stamp out this depraved and
> corrupt practice of robots having
> unnatural relationships with seafood...

A shaft of light atomises him.
CUT BACK TO: RINGO

> RINGO
>
> I thought you put your side of the
> argument very well. Anyway, where are
> we?

They are in an area with a curved floor which suggests a
centrifuge. Dotted around it are futuristic sarcophagi each
with its own elaborate life-support systems — like '2001'.

> RINGO
>
> There must be a notice somewhere.

They go up to the nearest sarcophagus. On the side of it is
an engraved plate which reads 'Starship Ron — B-fleet unit
three — pod seven — telephone sanitiser class four.'

> RINGO
> (Reading out plaque, emphasising the word 'Ron')
> Starship Ron — B-fleet unit three — pod
> seven — telephone sanitisor class four.
> That's funny, I once had a mate called that.

                              ROBOT
          What?

RINGO points to plaque, touches it.

                              RINGO
              Pod. He was a strange bloke.

As he touches it an alarm goes off, a very loud high-pitched
warbling siren sound. Lights flash, people in futuristic
costumes leap into action. SHOTS OF BRIDGE LIKE 'STAR TREK',
people have their fingers on buttons. SHOTS OF WARNING BOARD
with a series of lights which are marked 'red alert', 'blue
alert', 'mauve alert', 'russet alert', 'a sort of pinky
green alert', 'somewhere between beige and a very palish
yellow ochre alert' and 'not an alert at all'.
We see that 'Red alert' is flashing.
CUT BACK TO: RINGO talking to ROBOT

                              RINGO
              He wasn't christened Pod — his real
              name was Lonsdale Cowperthwaite. I
              never found out why.

They are grabbed from behind by paramilitary guards. One of
them touches ROBOT's arm, which lights up again with the
words 'erogenous zone'. ROBOT's face glows red again.

                              RINGO
              Look, can't you do something? (Notices
              ROBOT's embarrassment) Oh, that again.

They are quickly manacled together and they are surrounded
by some sort of coloured force field which immobilises them
in the postures they were last in. They are pushed along as
if they were a solid object.

                              RINGO
              Anyway, Pod used to go out with this
              bird called Helen.

                              ROBOT
          Oh?

> RINGO
>
> Anyway, I quite fancied her so we did a
> swap, I took Helen and he took my
> snorkel and flippers.

ZOOM IN on RINGO's face.

> RINGO
>
> She was my nest bird — and it's at
> times like this — you know, when I'm
> immobilised by some weird force field,
> and being pushed through the bowels of
> some enormous intergalactic spaceship
> full of mad second-hand car salesmen,
> that I like to think of her. Excuse me
> a moment.

His left arm comes across, unbolts and swings the front of
his body, which we now see to be hollow and open, as if it
were a box. CAMERA ZOOMS in on the darkness inside the box.
A point of light in the distance approaches as it grows
until we see it becomes RINGO and the Band.
THEY SING 'YOU'RE SIXTEEN'.
Then ZOOM onto black bass drum. Similarly, a point of light
grows into a full picture — A VISUAL SEQUENCE of RINGO with
a girl dressed in fifties-style costume.
END OF SONG.
PAN BACK OUT of RINGO's body. The Band is still visible on
Chroma-key. RINGO closes up his body.

By now they have arrived on the bridge of the starship. The
beam switches off at a signal from the CAPTAIN. RINGO and
ROBOT are released. The CAPTAIN is sitting in a chair, of
which we only see the back. It is a very large chair —
technical, futuristic, with switches, lights, t.v. screens
etc... A notice on the back says 'Captain'. Next to the
chair stands a clean-cut American, known as 'NUMBER 3'.

> NUMBER 3
> Captain, the intruders are here.

> CAPTAIN
> Well, gin and tonics all around then.

                    NUMBER 3
Shouldn't we interrogate them first?

                    CAPTAIN
Why? Don't they like gin and tonics?
Perhaps they'd prefer something else.

                    RINGO
No gin and tonic's fine.

                    ROBOT
That would be very nice.

                    NUMBER 3
No, I meant doing nasty things to them,
you know, torture. Putting match sticks
up their finger nails and so on to find
out their real mission.

                    CAPTAIN
Oh I doubt it, Number 3. I expect they
just popped in for a gin and tonic.

                    NUMBER 3
Oh come on, just a little bit of torture.

                    CAPTAIN
No, just ask them if they want ice and
lemon.

                    NUMBER 3
Alright. Do you want ice and lemon?

                    RINGO
        Er...

He doesn't make up his mind immediately. NUMBER 3 hits him
viciously.

                    NUMBER 3
Do you want ice and lemon?

                    RINGO
Er... Yes, that would be nice,

                     NUMBER 3

Cocktail biscuits?

                     RINGO

Er, yes please.

NUMBER 3 hits RINGO very viciously.

                     NUMBER 3

Any particular sort, or just a selection?

                     RINGO

Do you have any of those little salty
ones, shaped like a fish?

NUMBER 3 hits him again.

                     NUMBER 3

I'm asking the questions!

                     CAPTAIN

That'll do, Number 3. Just go ahead and
get them.

                     NUMBER 3

Very well gentlemen, but I shall be back.

He turns on his heel and makes as if to leave.

                     RINGO

Don't forget the biscuits.

NUMBER 3 turns back and knees RINGO in the groin.

                     RINGO
                (indicating ROBOT)

Don't forget him.

NUMBER 3 knees ROBOT in the groin and smashes his knee.
ROBOT hobbles around screaming with agony.

                     RINGO

And some of those olives with red
things in the middle.

NUMBER 3

Aah...

ROBOT turns on his beam and whacks NUMBER 3 on the head with it. NUMBER 3 exits, making 'Ouch!' noises. Then the CAPTAIN swings his chair round and we see him dressed as a very large and very realistic turkey. He pushes the head of the costume back and reveals his own head inside it — with a peaked cap on it.

CAPTAIN
Sorry about that, cutting legs off cats can be very tiring at times.

RINGO
Oh, is that what you've been doing?

CAPTAIN
What? Ah, no, it's Number 3. He's cutting legs off cats.

RINGO
Hadn't you better stop him?

CAPTAIN
What?

RINGO
Hadn't you better stop him.

CAPTAIN
Ah, I see! No, that's his nickname 'cutting legs off cats'.

RINGO
Oh I see. Well, that's very nice. Have you got a nickname?

CAPTAIN
Yes, we've all got nicknames. I'm known as 'sitting on rabbits'.

RINGO
You're 'sitting on rabbits'?

                    CAPTAIN
        Yes, but it's alright. I'm finished
        now.

He stands up. He picks up a flat and bloody rabbit from his
seat and throws it in a cupboard in which we see lots of
other dead rabbits.

                    RINGO
        But why are you dressed as a turkey?

                    CAPTAIN
        Oh it's just a little something the
        crew likes me to wear on Tuesdays.

                    RINGO
        Oh, it's still Tuesday is it then?

                    CAPTAIN
        Oh yes, it always has been. It will be
        for the next nine hundred years. You
        see, the amount of energy we need to
        travel at speeds approaching the speed
        of light is represented by the equation
        $E=MC^2$ over T, where E is energy, M is
        mass, C is the speed of light and T is
        Tuesday. Or is it time? No, T is
        Tuesday. Must be.

ROBOT whispers to RINGO.

                    CAPTAIN
        Is he alright?

                    RINGO
        Yes, he's just a bit shy recently.

                    CAPTAIN
        What did he say?

                    RINGO
        He said he thought it was the silliest
        starship he had ever been on.

                    CAPTAIN
        Ah, well you see it's a B ship. A sort
        of ark really, but a B-ark.

                    RINGO
        A B-ark?

                    CAPTAIN
        Yes, let me show you.

He pushes a button. We ZOOM up onto a t.v. screen which
shows the starship from the outside travelling through
space.

                    CAPTAIN
        Three hundred years ago you see, we
        were reliably informed that the planet
        Earth was dying, and so a mighty fleet
        of starships was built to set out and
        colonise new worlds. All the best
        brains of the world, the top
        scientists, creative geniuses, the great
        leaders of men were to be sent off in
        one fleet: the A fleet. Then the C
        fleet was going to contain all the
        people who did the actual work, and the
        B fleet — that's this — contained
        people who earned lots of money but
        didn't do much for anybody: the
        advertising executives, P.R. men, film
        producers, deodorant manufacturers,
        South Africans, the Osmonds, David
        Frost, politicians, bunny girls — you
        name it!

                    RINGO
        Second-hand car salesmen?

                    CAPTAIN
        Yes! Accountants.

                    RINGO
        Accountants are quite useful.

CAPTAIN

Yes, but they are so dull. Careers
advisors, telephone sanitisers — that
sort of person. Anyway, they were all
packed into this B fleet and we were
sent off first. (Pause) I've always had
my doubts about that.

RINGO

Eh, where are you all going?

CAPTAIN

Well, the ship's programmed to crash
straight into the sun.

RINGO

Won't you all be killed?

CAPTAIN

Yes, completely annihilated.

RINGO

Well what about you?

CAPTAIN

Er — oh, hadn't thought about that. Oh,
must be why they chose me. Cunning
bastards!

RINGO

Well? What are you going to do?

CAPTAIN

Have a large gin and tonic I think.

During the preceding dialogue we see on the t.v. screen
CLOSE-UPS of the pod doors on the spaceship. They are
decorated with horrible neon signs: 'Ron's garage', 'Dave's
diner', 'Haute Coiffure de Daryl', 'Hypermarket and Gun
Boutique', 'The Demented Dollar', 'Soft Core Porn', 'Klitty-
Klenz — the feminine tissue', 'Nazi: the real man's
hairspray'.
CUT BACK TO: STARSHIP BRIDGE. We see NUMBER 3 returning with
a mini army of paramilitary guards behind him.

                        NARRATOR
                         [V.O.]
          And so he decided to sing a song.

                         RINGO
          Ha! Call that narration?

                        NARRATOR
                         [V.O.]
          Well, I know it's not much, but it's
          all I'm obliged to do in the contract.

                         RINGO
          Look, from now on I'm doing my own
          narration. And so he sang a song.

                        NARRATOR
                         [V.O.]
          That's no good, that's what I said.

                         RINGO
          Look, shut up.

                        NARRATOR
                         [V.O.]
          Shan't.

                         RINGO
          I'll end the universe.

RINGO starts to wave his hand.

                        NARRATOR
                         [V.O.]
          Oh, I'd forgotten about that... Good
          morning.

CUT INTO: SONG 'STEP LIGHTLY'. The sequence is a Busby
Berkeley-style. All the characters are paramilitary guards.
MIX IN CLOSE-UPS of the Band where appropriate in the studio.
Then suddenly a beam of light appears besides the drums and
RINOG TRARS appears. He is identical to RINGO but is dressed
in a very futuristic space costume. He taps RINGO on the
shoulder.

> RINOG
>
> Excuse me, I think you've got some
> powers of mine.

> RINGO
>
> Are you Rinog Trars?

> RINOG
>
> Yes, and please can I have my powers
> back?

> RINGO
>
> We don't have to go into a lavatory do
> we?

> RINOG
>
> No.

> RINGO
>
> Fine, you can have them.

He holds up arm towards RINOG. There is an electric
discharge between them.

> RINGO
>
> There was a large metal person looking
> for you.

> RINGO
>
> What's happened to him?

> RINGO
>
> Well he went all coy over this
> crustacean, and now he's sitting in the
> spaceship waiting for a gin and tonic.

> RINOG
>
> Well, there's nothing wrong with that.

CUT TO: SENATE. Same scene as before, but two charred
bodies. Third senator standing and talking.

                        SENATOR #3
              ...and stamp out this abominable
              practice of Robots drinking gin and
              tonics on spaceships.

A beam of light, same as before, disintegrates SENATOR #3.
CUT BACK TO: RINGO and RINOG — studio scene. We see that
RINOG still has a beam of light coming out of his eyes.

                        RINGO
              That's been done. Have you seen this
              one?

He lays out three cards on the drums.

                        RINGO
              Find the Queen.

                        RINOG
              No, I've got to be going.

                        RINGO
              I think I'll stay here. You don't get
              hit, I'll play you out.

Into introduction of 'Goodnight Vienna'.

                        RINOG
              Cheers and thanks for the powers.

                        RINGO
              Anytime.

RINGO picks up the vocals on 'Goodnight Vienna'. We see him
and the Band playing the song. Behind them we see RINOG
walking towards a large flying saucer. He is joined by
ROBOT, who is still blushing because he has PRAWN on his
arm, wearing a wedding dress. Gladiators, customs officials,
etc... — the entire cast — all enter the flying saucer which
starts to ascend. RINOG stands in the doorway of the saucer
and we see the rest of the cast crouched behind him. RINGO
waves to RINOG from the ground.

                    RINGO
          Goodbye Rinog, it was nice meeting you.

                    RINOG
          Goodbye Ringo.

RINOG starts to wave. There is an immediate very loud
explosion and the screen goes blank.

                    RINGO
                    [V.O.]
          You shouldn't have done that.

                    RINOG
                    [V.O.]
          Oh, I forgot about that. Sorry.
          Universe.

THE CLOSING CREDITS CAN BE SEEN OVER THIS LAST NUMBER.

THE END

JAKE'S JOURNEY

As conceived and written by Graham and his long-time companion and collaborator, David Sherlock, *Jake's Journey* was going to be a television first: the first original primetime American sitcom ever written and produced in another country. The series was initiated by a phone call to Graham from Allan McKeown at Witzend Productions. What was proposed was an American television sitcom to be loosely based on Mark Twain's book, *A Connecticut Yankee in The Court of King Arthur*. While Graham was initially reluctant, he did eventually agree to re-read Twain's book and have a think. "I never had fantasies about writing an American sitcom," Graham once said, "but then I thought, 'Hang on, if they want to pay me *that* much money to write twenty-three minutes of material which probably won't get made anyway... why not?'"

In the end Graham agreed to the initial concept, but said that he and David wanted more flexibility with the story and characters and so they introduced elements of time travel, *Alice in Wonderland* and even *The Once and Future King* into the story.

Graham enthused, "That's when it all started to get interesting. We now had the freedom to go forward or backwards in time, to go to other planets... the possibilities were endless."

A concept meeting between the Chapman/Sherlock team and CBS-TV was set up in Los Angeles while Graham was on tour, but he and David soon discovered to their utter horror that instead of it being a general chat about the show, they were expected to read out actual pages of dialogue. Of course, nothing had been written so they huddled together in their hotel room and furiously jotted down ideas. What they ended up with was about ten minutes of strong material which got lots of laughs from the assembled suits at CBS. A pilot was commissioned (to be scripted by Graham and David) and a budget of $1.5 million dollars was set. Filming was to begin in London, for CBS-TV, in 1987.

Directing the pilot was the late Hal Ashby, who had also directed the late Peter Sellers in one of last great films, *Being There*. The title role of Jake went to Chris Young (of *Max Headroom*), with cameo appearances by Peter Cook as the King, and Liz Smith (the elderly mother in *A Private Function*) as the Witch. Graham had only intended to write the series, but when the pivotal role of Sir George remained uncast some three weeks into filming, he agreed to don the rusty armour and play the part himself. "I secretly loved it," he said, "although I never let on." Graham eventually ended up playing both the part of Sir George and the Queen who only says "Good evening."

Soon after the pilot episode was completed, *Jake's Journey* immediately ran into problems. CBS took a look and decided not to pick up the series after all. It's rumoured that while every junior executive at the network loved the show and lobbied hard for it's inclusion, Lawrence Tisch then president of CBS didn't understand the concept and took an extreme dislike to it. Unfazed, Graham and company took matters into their own hands and began to shop the tape around. After ABC-TV showed strong interest, CBS decided to take another look and thought that yes, they would commission more episodes after all. Work began again on the series. In addition to the pilot, two other episodes were scripted and several other script concepts were put into development.

Then CBS had yet another change of heart. They decided that no, on further reflection, they didn't want the series after all. So *Jake's Journey* was shopped around again on the open market. In the end, The Disney Channel decided to pick up the series but, just as things began to look up, Graham fell ill with the throat cancer that would eventually claim his life. The show was again placed on the shelf. This time it would not be revived.

This script (the pilot episode) was produced by Marc Merson and Allan McKeown for Witzend Productions. It was filmed, but never aired.

JAKE'S JOURNEY

By Graham Chapman and David Sherlock

©1988 Graham Chapman and David Sherlock

ACT ONE

FADE IN:

OPENING TITLES

A MONTAGE of STILLS which will in quick order show us: a
suburban American home, complete with cycles, basketball
board and barbecue. The FAMILY posed in front of the house.
Various SHOTS of packing, with various reactions from
members of the family: MIKE, determined, JEAN, a mixture of
cheerful and sad, SARAH, excited and JAKE resigned to a fate
worse than death, trying to pack all his stuff. Saying
goodbye to the house. In an insanely overloaded American
taxi, various reactions. Plane taking off. London airport.
In an insanely overloaded English taxi, again buried by
bags. Some SHOTS of London sights, JAKE and OTHERS staring
at them. Their new home in suburban London, going in the
door, posing for a MATCHING SHOT in front of the house.

DISSOLVE TO:

EXT. SIBLEY'S HOUSE. DAY (EARLY MORNING)

ESTABLISHING SHOT of a spacious, half-timbered old house in
the London suburbs. A MILKMAN leaves a couple of pints of
milk on the doorstep and goes on.

INT. SIBLEY'S KITCHEN. DAY (EARLY MORNING)

There's a large dining table in one end of the kitchen. MIKE
sits at the table, reading a newspaper as SARAH, 12, sets
the table and JEAN finishes making breakfast.

                    JEAN
        I have a surprise...
                    (Calling)
        Jake, hurry up!

                    MIKE
        What surprise?

                         JEAN
         I'm making our first traditional
         English breakfast.

JAKE comes in. He's wearing slacks, a blazer and an askew
tie and puts down, a school satchel. He's not a happy boy.

                         MIKE
         Good morning, Jake!

                         JAKE
                    (glumly)
         Morning.

JAKE sits down.

                         JEAN
         Straighten your tie, dear.

                         JAKE
         Why do I have to dress like this to go
         to school?

                         MIKE
         That's how it's done in England, Jake.

                         JAKE
         I feel like I work for IBM.

                         JEAN
         You'll get used to it. Are you making
         friends at school?

                         JAKE
         Friends are what I had back in Dayton.
         Scott, Jack, Kirk — I've known them
         since we were all ten. I don't know
         anybody here and I never will.

                         MIKE
                    (behind newspaper)
         That's the spirit.

                         SARAH
          You know Elizabeth Feverton. Or you'd
          like to.

                         JAKE
          Shut up.

                         JEAN
          Who is Elizabeth Feverton?

                         JAKE
          She lives down the street, I haven't
          talked to her, I've only seen her.

                         SARAH
          You mean stared at her. He was
          practically drooling.

                         JAKE
          An accident can be arranged, you know.

JEAN puts down full plates in front of JAKE, MIKE and SARAH.
JAKE stares down at his for a long beat.

                         JAKE
          You're not serious.

                         JEAN
          It's kippers! Traditional English
          breakfast.

JAKE looks back down at his plate.

Kippers, eggs, boiled tomato. EXTREME CLOSE-UP of the
kippers.

BACK TO SCENE
                         JAKE
          Mom, it's 7.30 in the morning. I can't
          eat something that's looking back at me.

                         MIKE
          Don't judge it before you try it, Jake.
          Keep an open mind.

JAKE prods a kipper gingerly. MIKE takes a forkful of his.

                    MIKE
Mmm — terrific!

                    JEAN
If you think you might like this
Elizabeth, why don't you talk to her?
Call her up, invite her over.

                    JAKE
No way.

                    MIKE
You called girls when we were in the
States.

                    JAKE
They don't do that stuff here. It's all
coats and ties and...
               (with accent)
...'I'm terribly, terribly pleased to
meet you'. I wouldn't know what to say.
She'd think I was from Mars.

                    JEAN
No she wouldn't. You're a nice-looking
boy...

                    SARAH
Him? Yuck! She'd puke if he called her.

                    JAKE
Nobody asked you.

                    JEAN
Nothing ventured, nothing gained. You've
got to get over being tongued-tied...

JAKE, upset, stands up.

                              JAKE
          I'd love to have everybody pick on me
          for another hour or two, but if I don't
          leave I'll be late for school.

                              JEAN
          You haven't touched your food.

                              JAKE
          Sorry, but I don't want to find out
          what happens when you're tardy here. I
          think they flog you.

                              MIKE
          I'll walk with you.

INT. LIVING ROOM. DAY

JAKE and MIKE walk through the living room. JAKE carries his
school satchel.

                              MIKE
          Jake, I have to tell you I'm not
          thrilled with your attitude about being
          here.

                              JAKE
          And I'm not thrilled with being here. I
          didn't ask to come. Today the Indians
          are playing a double-header with the
          Yankees and there isn't a person in
          this country who cares!

INT. FRONT HALL. DAY

JAKE and MIKE walk through.

                              MIKE
          Well, you have to find English things
          you like.

                              JAKE
          Like kippers? Look me in the eye and
          tell me you liked them.

MIKE thinks for a beat.

> MIKE
>
> They're the worst thing I've ever
> eaten. But the point is, I tried them.
> Jake, don't be so scared to take a
> chance. Call this Elizabeth. You've got
> to think of life as an adventure.

EXT. FRONT DOOR OF HOUSE, DAY

MIKE stays at the front door as JAKE starts down the walk.

> MIKE
>
> Keep that in mind, Jake. An adventure!
> You're young, you're healthy, and
> you're in London!

> JAKE
> (unenthused)
> Right.

EXT. WALK. DAY

JAKE approaches a hedge that leads to a common. He looks
down and mutters to himself. CAMERA MOVES IN CLOSE on his
face as he goes through the hedge.

> JAKE
> (mimicking his father)
> 'Call this Elizabeth. Think of life as
> an adventure. You're in London!' Well,
> I don't want to be in London!

As JAKE emerges from the hedge, there is the sound of
clattering hooves. JAKE frowns and looks up. His eyes widen
in horror.

EXT. GREENSWARD. DAY

JAKE'S P.O.V.

A medieval knight on horseback (SIR GEORGE) thunders toward
us, his lance directly at the camera.

JAKE looks down at himself; he is dressed as a medieval
page. In his hand, instead of his satchel, he holds a pole,
at the end of which hangs a pendulous brown bag (a pig's
bladder full of gore).

> SIR GEORGE
>
> Hold it steady!

JAKE looks around to see if there's some way out, but all he
sees is an excrementally idyllic English country glade. As SIR
GEORGE gets close, JAKE reflexively pulls the bladder out of the
way. As SIR GEORGE goes by, there is a shout of 'Whoa!', a
clattering crash, and a cry for help from SIR GEORGE.

> SIR GEORGE
>
> Help me up, then lad! Don't just stand
> there!

JAKE looks around and realises that this means him and goes
to help. SIR GEORGE may have been impressive thirty years
earlier, but now he lies helpless in rusty and battered
armour with be-draggled plumes.

> SIR GEORGE
>
> I told you to hold that bladder in
> front of you! Hold it to the side.
> You've ruined a perfectly good pair of
> second-hand hose.

JAKE helps him up. JAKE is still in shock from the sudden
switch.

> JAKE
>
> Where am I? What's going on?

SIR GEORGE cuffs him smartly on the back of the neck.

> SIR GEORGE
>
> People who ask questions like that
> never have adventures.

> JAKE
> (rubbing his neck)
> What did you do that for?

He is cuffed again.

> SIR GEORGE
> Good question. Bright lad. Well, it's
> just tradition, I suppose.

> JAKE
> Oh.

He is cuffed again.

> SIR GEORGE
> Never did me any harm.

> JAKE
> Why did you do it again?

He cuffs him again.

> SIR GEORGE
> I'm obliged to, if you answer back.

> JAKE
> What if I don't answer back?

He is cuffed again.

> SIR GEORGE
> You always do.

JAKE begins to speak but holds back, realising the rules of
the game.

> SIR GEORGE
> Pages always answer back, otherwise
> it's construed as dumb insolence.
> (He pauses)
> Are you being dumb and insolent?
> (JAKE shakes his head vigorously)
> Good lad. Well done!

> JAKE
> Thank you.

He is cuffed again.

>   SIR GEORGE
>   They always do. Now, about our quest...

They are walking beside the horse toward a dark wood.

>   SIR GEORGE
>   I have here a love letter of such
>   overblown sentimentality that I have
>   used it twice as an emetic.
>   (he taps a moth-eaten scroll)
>   It's from Prince Kevin the Rich. He
>   thought he might not be rich enough to
>   land this very rich Princess, so he's
>   gone off on a crusade or two, and gave
>   me this proposal of marriage. We have to
>   brave many hazards, dragons, etc...
>   etc... and deliver it to his beloved,
>   the Princess Yeugh.
>   (pronounced as in throwing up)
>   That's our quest.

>   JAKE
>   Our quest? My quest is to get the heck
>   out of here! I have to get to school —
>   to my family!

SIR GEORGE cuffs him.

>   JAKE
>   Will you cut that out?

>   SIR GEORGE
>   You mean you don't like it?

>   JAKE
>   No! I don't like it.

>   SIR GEORGE
>   You should have said. Now where was I? The
>   rules say clearly it's only one quest at a
>   time. So the Princess is who we're after.

                    JAKE
        If we find her and deliver the message,
        will you help me then?

                    SIR GEORGE
        Naturally... that's what I do.

                    JAKE
        Okay, you're on... tell me, who is this
        Princess Yeugh. That's the ugliest name
        I've ever heard.

                    SIR GEORGE
        She's called Yeugh because her parents
        thought it would be character-forming.
        But she is a princess, and therefore
        pretty. I imagine she's the usual
        curvaceous blonde with pert, shapely...
            (He notices JAKE's keen interest)
        ...ears.

In an explosion of green light and a billow of purple smoke,
a WITCH appears in front of them. She is apparently unaware
that her face has been blackened by the explosions and that
the hem of her garment is on fire.

                    WITCH
        Come in!

                    SIR GEORGE
        What do you mean 'come in'? We can't
        come in, we're all out.

                    WITCH
        Well, if you're all out, I'm not in.
        Good day to you.

She raises her wand and begins a witch-like cackle. She
notices the flames.

                    WITCH
        Oh, damn!
            (She starts to beat them out)
        Oh damn, damn, damn!

> (she runs, jumps and sits in a nearby
> stream, putting out the flames)
> Sorry about that. I'll get it right
> next time. Have a nice day.

She disappears. SIR GEORGE shrugs and they begin to walk on
into the woods.

                    SIR GEORGE
          I wonder what that was about? Witches
          don't usually appear for nothing.

Suddenly, hovering in front of them is the disembodied head
of the WITCH.

                    WITCH'S HEAD
          Oh! Nearly forgot... had a note for
          you... got burnt... just says 'to whom
          it.' Will there be a reply?

Blank looks all around.

                    SIR GEORGE
          How can we reply if we don't know what
          it says?

                    WITCH
          Wouldn't stop me.

SIR GEORGE cuffs her automatically.

                    WITCH
          Ow! Alright, alright, it said 'Beware!'

                    SIR GEORGE
          Beware what?

                    WITCH
          Just... 'Beware!!!'

                    SIR GEORGE
          That's not particularly useful, is it?
          Didn't it even say what we have to
          beware of?

                          WITCH
            No. A dragon, I suppose. Beware.
            Beware!!! Have a nice day.

The WITCH emits a horrible cackle. She begins to disappear.
There is a flash of green light and the cackle degenerates
into yelps of pain.

                          JAKE
            Wait! Can you help me get out of here?

Too late — she's gone.

                          SIR GEORGE
            Keep your eyes open for a dragon.

                          JAKE
            I don't believe in dragons! ...On the
            other hand, I just asked a witch for
            advice...

                          SIR GEORGE
            You're quite right, lad, dragons is
            abstract. They are a metaphor for some
            unspeakable 'orror. We have been warned,
            badly, but warned. So we'll have to
            look out.

They walk on.

                          SIR GEORGE
            The road to the castle crosses a stream
            around here. Unfortunately, there's a
            troll bridge.

                          JAKE
            We have to pay?

SIR GEORGE stops, sits down on a nearby tree stump and takes
his lunch out of his helmet.

                          SIR GEORGE
            Right. That's it. I'm not going any
            further with you.

                    JAKE
What have I done?

                    SIR GEORGE
That was a blatant attempt at a pun.
The second lowest form of wit. You
heard perfectly well. It's a bridge
guarded by a troll, it's not a 'toll
bridge'. I won't move until you
apologise.

                    JAKE
I misheard. Honestly. Sorry.

They walk along the bank of the stream again.

                    JAKE
What is a troll?

                    SIR GEORGE
Well, it's a sort of huge, pointy,
fierce, hairy, slimy greenish,
uncooperative entity which eats people
— smaller people. Anyone under five
foot eight.

                    JAKE
That's very specific.

                    SIR GEORGE
They are, no more than you not liking
eggplant. Do you like eggplant?

                    JAKE
No.

                    SIR GEORGE
Well, there you are. How tall are you?

                    JAKE
Five eight and a quarter. With shoes.

                    SIR GEORGE
Shoes don't count.

                    JAKE
          Wait a minute! This thing will eat me
          if we try to cross the bridge!

                    SIR GEORGE
          Unless we distract it in some way. It's
          alright. I have a plan.

Round a bend in the river we can see a crude wooden bridge.
We are now in the depth of the forest. It is dark and misty.
There is the sound of ominous heavy breathing. The whole
effect is eerie. The heavy breathing culminates in an
appalling smoker's-type coughing fit and we can now make out
the murky and forbidding figure of the TROLL blocking the
bridge. A young PEASANT carrying a bundle of kindling wood
steps onto the bridge. He walks quite bravely up to within a
few feet of the TROLL and tries his luck.

                    PEASANT
                   (pointing)
          Look out — behind you!

The TROLL wearily shakes his head with a 'not that old one
again' expression and knocks him violently sideways into the
river with a casual blow of the forearm.

                    TROLL
          Huh, what a life. I've been knocking
          people into this river and eating them
          for twenty-eight, no, thirty years...
          and what do I get? 'Look out, there's
          someone behind you!' Huh, there must be
          more to life than this. What have I got
          to look forward to? Another thirty
          years of knocking people in a river. It
          doesn't bear thinking about.

                    JAKE
          Sounds like my father.

                    SIR GEORGE
          Yes, middle-age I suppose. Just a
          phase.

                        JAKE
          How do we get round him?

                        SIR GEORGE
          You should know that — distract him.

                        JAKE
          Wait a minute, I thought you had a
          plan.

                        SIR GEORGE
          That is the plan. Now go.

          JAKE edges onto the bridge.

                        JAKE
          Good morning!

                        TROLL
          You talking to me?

                        JAKE
          Yes, nice day, isn't it?

                        TROLL
          Is it?

                        JAKE
          Yeah, sure is.
          (pause)
          I thought there was supposed to be a
          troll round here.

                        TROLL
                      (guardedly)
          Yesss.

                        JAKE
          Huh, well glad there isn't.

                        TROLL
          What do you mean?

> JAKE

Oh, I was expecting to find some vile old nasty foul-smelling beast.

> TROLL

Were you?

> JAKE

Must have gone, oh well, nice meeting you.

> TROLL

Thank you.

> JAKE

Like that shirt.

> TROLL

Shirt?

> JAKE

Your shirt. Brilliant.

> TROLL

What, this...?

> JAKE

Yeah, real trendy. Where did you get it?

> TROLL

I've had it for years.

> JAKE

Nah! And who did the hair?

> TROLL

What do you mean?

> JAKE

It's great!!!

> TROLL

What do you mean, 'great'?

                              JAKE
                Well, it's spiky. Looks good.

                              TROLL
                No... Do you think it does?

                              JAKE
                Come on, did you have it cut round
                here?

                              TROLL
                No, it just sort of grows like this.

SIR GEORGE proffers his burnished shield which JAKE hands to
the TROLL as a mirror.

                              JAKE
                You're lucky. Couldn't do that with
                mine.

The TROLL begins to primp and preen.

                              TROLL
                Mmm, it is different.

                              JAKE
                Different? It's fantastic...

                              TROLL
                Well, I suppose it is a bit fantastic.
                Certainly not ordinary...

As the TROLL preens even more, SIR GEORGE and JAKE steal
past and away.

                              TROLL
                ...Not ordinary. It is unusual...
                better than anyone's in this forest.
                Yeah, he's got something... trendy, eh?
                Huh, imagine...

As we follow JAKE and SIR GEORGE stealing away, we hear:

> TROLL
> (V.O.)
> What a nice young man.

Then the sound of PEASANT #2.

> PEASANT #2
> (V.O.)
> Look out behind you!

There is a scream, a thump, a splash and a laugh.

> TROLL
> (V.O.)
> Huh, I feel like a snack.

The terrible noises of the snack being consumed recede as JAKE and SIR GEORGE move off into the forest.

> SIR GEORGE
> Well done — you did well.

> JAKE
> I did, didn't I? I took a chance and it paid off...

> SIR GEORGE
> Right. So much for the easy part. Now things begin to get tricky.

On JAKE's reaction, we FADE OUT

END OF ACT ONE

ACT TWO

FADE IN:

EXT. FOREST. DAY

JAKE and SIR GEORGE follow a trail that leads to a clearing.
They are in mid-conversation.

>   JAKE
>   So I guess most quests end in success,
>   right? I mean, knights and pages don't
>   usually get killed, right?

>   SIR GEORGE
>   No, as a rule they just lose the odd
>   limb or two...
>   (he spots a building ahead)
>   ...Ah! An inn! They should be able to
>   direct us to the castle.

They go toward the inn.

The sign shows a picture of a prince and dragon and reads
'The Prince and Metaphor'.

INT. THE PRINCE AND METAPHOR. DAY

The interior is primitive medieval. There is a fire in the
middle of the room and no chimney, just a hole in the roof.
Three-legged stools surround a crude refectory table, pigs,
chickens and dogs roam around freely. The LANDLORD is busy
pouring ale for one of the few customers. A COUPLE of
MINSTRELS add to the pub atmosphere by playing the flute and
tabor. SIR GEORGE strides up to the table and bangs on it to
attract the LANDLORD's attention.

>   SIR GEORGE
>   Landlord! Can you tell us the
>   whereabouts of Castle Grede?

The music stops. The LANDLORD freezes at the mention of this
name. Everyone in the place, including chickens and dogs,
falls silent and looks furtively around them. PEOPLE cross
themselves.

> LANDLORD
> Never heard of it! No castle of that
> name round these parts. And if you'd
> take my advice, sir, you'd steer well
> clear of it even if there was. There be
> horrific tales of gruesome things
> happening to all who enter therein, if
> they do...

More PEOPLE cross themselves.

> LANDLORD
> ...And it's terrible for trade.

(Claps hand to mouth.)

> SIR GEORGE
> This non-existent castle... would it be
> about a mile away?

> LANDLORD
> No, but if it were there, that's where
> it would be.

> JAKE
> If the castle was there, why would it
> be so dangerous?

> LANDLORD
> Some people might tell you, that scores
> of princes have gone there, all suitors
> to Princess Yeugh, and that none of
> them has ever come back. All eaten by
> the dragon. But nothing could be
> further from the truth. I've told you
> too much already.

> SIR GEORGE
> Well, that's your opinion.

> (to room in general)
> Can anyone tell me the way to Castle
> Grede? I have a message for the
> Princess Yeugh.

More crossing and muttering. SIR GEORGE sees a strange
COUPLE at the other end of the table.

> SIR GEORGE
>
> Let's ask them.

> JAKE
>
> But they're lobsters!

> SIR GEORGE
>
> Don't be prejudiced.

They move over to where TWO LOBSTERS, wearing the latest
(1988) aerodynamic cycling clothes, sit. They are enormous,
human-being sized lobsters. Their ultra-fast looking
machines are propped up against the table.

> LOBSTER #1
> (in a nasal voice)
> Excuse me, maybe we can help. We're
> only touring, but we do have a map.

SIR GEORGE grabs the map and begins to look at it. The
LOBSTER #2 talks to JAKE.

> LOBSTER #2
> (also in a nasal voice)
> Are either of you princes?

> JAKE
>
> No.

> LOBSTER #2
>
> Pity. They won't let you in then.

> JAKE
>
> If we say we're princes, how will they
> find out we're not?

                    LOBSTER #2
        Torture.

                         JAKE
                      (nodding)
                  That would work.

                    LOBSTER #2
        They wouldn't let us in, either.

                    LOBSTER #1
                 (looking up from map)
        May have been the bikes... and your
        shorts don't leave much to the
        imagination.

                    LOBSTER #2
                   (ignoring this)
        Though why anyone wants to see the
        Princess, I don't know. I'm told
        facially she's got as much going for
        her as the average prawn.

                         JAKE
                   (to SIR GEORGE)
        You said she was beautiful.

                      SIR GEORGE
        Chivalry.
                   (Puts down the map)
        Thank you. Right! To the castle!

EXT. WOODLAND APPROACH TO CASTLE. DAY

                      SIR GEORGE
        It's that way.

                         JAKE
        How do you know?

SIR GEORGE nods to the side of the road. JAKE looks. There's
a billboard reading:
'Princes (rich) this way'
...and an arrow pointing the direction.

EXT. DRAWBRIDGE TO CASTLE GREDE. DAY

A rather grand stall advertises 'Expensive betrothal gifts —
no bargains'. Another displays 'Princessly Requisites' and
yet another stall sells 'Last Wills and Testaments'. As JAKE
and SIR GEORGE walk up to a HUGE GUARD at their end of the
drawbridge, a deadish-looking princely PERSON tied into
knots in his armour (the tangled heap of armour has a
coronet on top) is carried out on a crude stretcher and
unceremoniously tipped over.

                    SIR GEORGE
          We would like to see the Princess
          Yeugh.

                        GUARD
          Are you princes?

                    SIR GEORGE
          Well, not as the term is usually
          defined, but —

                    HUGE GUARD
          Shove off.

JAKE confidently steps in front of SIR GEORGE and smiles.

                        JAKE
          That chain-mail shirt looks terrific.

                    HUGE GUARD
          Thank you.

EXT. BANK OF CASTLE MOAT. DAY

                    SIR GEORGE
          Good try, well done. Don't worry, we'll
          find another way in.

EXT. CASTLE MOAT. DAY

SIR GEORGE and JAKE sit in a coracle (a small round boat) on
the moat at the rear of the castle.

                    SIR GEORGE
          I was thinking. You've been a very good
          page, and I thought I ought to reward
          you. I have decided to honour you by
          allowing you to complete this quest.

                    JAKE
               Why me? It's dangerous.

                    SIR GEORGE
          Of course it is. It's a quest! You
          can't become a Knight unless you've
          been on a quest or two. Just follow
          directions.

SIR GEORGE stands up in the unsteady boat. He takes out a
grappling hook and rope from his voluminous cloak.
Skillfully he twirls the hook round at the end of the rope
and then launches it vertically upwards toward a turret
which overhangs the rest of the wall above them. It sails up
neatly through a drainage hole beneath the turret, catches
and grips firmly.

                    JAKE
          That was very good.

                    SIR GEORGE
          I am a Knight.

SIR GEORGE tucks the scroll beneath Jake's tabard and
bustles him into standing and holding onto the rope.

                    SIR GEORGE
          All you have to do is climb up the
          rope, find the Princess and read that
          to her. I'll drop in later if I have a
          chance. Climb, climb!

                    JAKE
          You don't understand. I flunked P.E.! I
          can't go up there —

                    SIR GEORGE
          You could, with encouragement.

With a forceful stroke of the paddle, SIR GEORGE moves the
small boat out from underneath JAKE. JAKE hangs onto the
rope, staring down at the cold and ominously dark water. SIR
GEORGE paddles away.

                        SIR GEORGE
          Good luck.

                        JAKE
          If I live, I'll get you for this!

JAKE struggles to start climbing.

INT. THE DUNGEON AREA. DAY

JAKE climbs up to the grappling hook which has secured
itself on the stone rim of a sluice inside the room. His
head pops out and he looks around as sees that he is in a
central chamber of the dungeon area. There are barred and
shuttered doors all around the room. Occasional shrieks and
moans of agony are heard from behind them. One door bears a
sign saying 'Nothing by Mouth Ever'.

In the middle of the room at a trestle table sit a COUPLE of
TORTURER's WIVES — yuppies of their period. They chat as
they polish a pile of thumbscrews, not noticing JAKE.

                        WIFE #1
               I've got five of his shirts in soak at
               the moment. It's that new Iron Maiden.
               When that closes up on someone, you get
               much more spattering than you did with
               the old ones...

                        WIFE #2
               Don't I know it. We've got three of
               them. It spurts everywhere. But then
               it's more a deterrent, isn't it?

As JAKE ducks and darts his way across the room unseen, we
continue to hear the conversation.

                        WIFE #1
               Well, we've got more on order... six I

think; and we've got four new dungeons.
Really nice... ever so cramped and damp
and slimy and smelly, and they've been
built with racks en-suite.

                    WIFE #2
Our eight new dungeons with racks en-
suite have specially imported Sicilian
slime.

                    WIFE #1
Oh, absolutely! We have Sicilian slime
piped through to all our dungeons.
Don't know how we coped without it.

Into the room comes the HEAD TORTURER, who wears a mask and
a bloody leather apron over blood-bespattered shirt and
breeches. He speaks to his WIFE. We hear their exchange as
JAKE continues his way through the room, darting behind
torture devices to avoid being seen.

                 HEAD TORTURER
Sorry love, I'll be a bit late for
lunch. Got an emergency rack job on...
Hello, Mrs Gantlet, how's Buddy then,
busy?

                    WIFE #2
Up to his knees in eyeballs... Still,
mustn't grumble.

                 HEAD TORTURER
Not when the work's coming in.

He takes off the spattered shirt, adds it to the heap near
the tubs and puts on a clean one handed to him by WIFE #1.

                    WIFE #1
Who's on the rack?

                 HEAD TORTURER
Oh, just some git found wandering round
the castle. Said he'd lost his way, ha
ha ha!

His WIFE joins in with knowing laughter. JAKE reacts.

> HEAD TORTURER
> Pull my other leg, I said. I'm going to
> stretch both of yours.

JAKE is out in the open just as the HEAD TORTURER starts to
turn toward him. JAKE has no choice but to open the nearest
door and go in.

INT. BAVARIAN DRAWING ROOM. DAY[1]

When JAKE comes in, he is now dressed as a Tyrolean youth,
with lederhosen, bib, etc... He finds himself at the front
of an audience made up of BAVARIAN LADIES listening to a
STRING QUARTET composed of high-ranking Nazi officers in SS
uniforms. They play a sprightly Mozart piece. JAKE spots SIR
GEORGE at the far end of the room, dressed in leather knee
breeches, a loden jacket, and Tyrolean hat. SIR GEORGE
gestures for JAKE to come to the door at the back. As JAKE
walks along, his shoes squeak. The BAVARIAN LADIES in unison
swivel their heads and glare at him. He smiles nervously and
goes on. At the end of the room, SIR GEORGE opens the door
and lets JAKE through.

INT. VAULTED CHAMBER. DAY

JAKE backs in — he's back in medieval page's garb. He bumps
in to a SERVANT sweeping up some bits of clothing. JAKE
turns to face the SERVANT, who shakes his head wearily.

> SERVANT
> Beryl! We've got another one.

> BERYL
> (O.S.)
> Oh no! There's no more room in the bin.

---

[1] Not too surprisingly considering this was to be a primetime American sitcom (circa 1988), this scene
was later cut from the finished pilot. According to Graham, it was inserted merely to show that Jake
and Sir George were capable of travelling to any time, not just the medieval period.

                    SERVANT
          Well, prod them down a bit, then sit on
          the lid.
                    (to JAKE)
          I'll tell the Royals you're here.
          They'll be with you presently.

He starts to go out.

                    JAKE
              (holding onto the scroll)
          I only came to leave this note! You
          don't need to bother them.

But the SERVANT has gone, locking another door behind him.
From O.S. we hear a shout

                    SERVANT
                    (O.S.)
          There's another one!

While JAKE re-examines the chamber for a means of escape,
the KING and QUEEN enter. Because of their chatting, they do
not notice him at first. The QUEEN has an amazingly small
mouth.

                    KING
          That last one showed promise until he
          allowed himself to be strewn around the
          room like that.

                    QUEEN
          Good evening.

                    KING
          Ah, there you are!

                    JAKE
          Good afternoon.

                    KING
          Hello.

                          QUEEN
        Good evening.

                          KING
                        (to JAKE)
        Now, open wide.

                          JAKE
        I'm sorry?

                          KING
        Open your mouth wide.

JAKE, at a loss, does so. The KING takes out a pair of
calipers and measures the width of his mouth.

                          KING
        Hmm... two and a quarter. A bit
        generous I'm afraid.

                          JAKE
        Generous?

                          KING
        Mmm yes. Not a particularly greedy
        mouth at all. You're borderline, but
        we'll let you carry on.

                          QUEEN
                        (nodding)
        Good evening.

                          JAKE
        Er... could you explain, please?

                          KING
        Of course. I explain the courtship
        procedure to all the princes. You...

                          JAKE
        I am not a...

                          KING
        Quiet, I'm expounding my theory!

                         QUEEN
                       (sternly)
Good evening!

                          KING
You see, we are ludicrously rich, and
certainly the greediest people in this
Kingdom. My wife is so greedy, she
restricts herself to only ever saying
the words 'good evening' because she is
terrified of giving anything away.

                         QUEEN
                  (nods in agreement)
Good evening.

                          KING
You see, I made a scientific study of
family trees. In all the wealthiest
families, where both partners are
greedy; they have greedy offspring. But
if one of the partners is even slightly
generous, then three out of four of
their children will be wantonly
spendthrift.

                         QUEEN
                   (shaking head)
Good evening.

                          KING
So, for the wealth of our children's
children, we have made it known that
our daughter is physically repellent,
to attract only the right type. Then if
they pass the mean mouth test, they go
on to the final; where they have to
prove themselves greedy enough to
overcome extreme fear. Just wait here,
our daughter will be with you in a
moment. Good afternoon.

He leaves.

                         QUEEN
                        (sweetly)
            Good evening.

She leaves.

                         JAKE
            Extreme fear? Listen, this test —
            couldn't you make it an essay question?

JAKE scrabbles at the door they have locked behind them. It
is completely unyielding. He checks out the window and sees
a horrendous drop. He goes over to the stone pier and
examines the bars. While he is examining the bars where they
attach to the wall, he hears a noise behind the door at the
back of the pier and flattens himself against the wall. The
PRINCESS YEUGH, stunningly beautiful, but demurely veiled,
enters, and descends the steps, peering around the room
ahead of her.

                         PRINCESS
            Hello? ...Hello?
                        (sees no prince)
            Oh, bother.

She puts her veil back up and lifts her skirts to climb the
steps back to the door through which she came.

JAKE, who was previously happy to remain crouching flat
against the wall, as inconspicuous as possible, now stands
openly admiring her beauty.

                         JAKE
            Princess Yeugh?

                         PRINCESS
            Yes. You must be the Prince.

                         JAKE
            Well, I have...

He draws out the scroll...

PRINCESS

Oooh!

JAKE

Um.

They are struck dumb by each other's charms.

PRINCESS

Ah! ...Oh.

The enthralled JAKE gathers inspiration and passion as he addresses her.

JAKE

I have, er... something to read to you.
(He unscrolls the parchment scroll only
to find that the letter has washed off)
Oh, I don't need that. If it had any
sense it would have said that you're
the most beautiful girl ever. I've
never met anyone like you — not even at
the Dayton Mall. A guy would risk any
adventure for you.

PRINCESS

Oh lovely! You won't mind the wolves a
bit. Super!
(shouts through the door)
Mummy, Daddy, I think this may be the
one.

KING

(from outside)
Alright, here come the wolves!

JAKE

Wolves?

PRINCESS

Daddy's pets. They've been trained to
savage, maul and mutilate anyone except
my true prince.

                        JACK
        But I'm not a prince

                        PRINCESS
        Not a prince?

                        JACK
        No. The message I brought was from
        Prince Kevin the Rich. I'm just Jake
        Sibley from Dayton, Ohio.

                        PRINCESS
        Not a prince, but very cute. Oh, good.
        Daddy, cancel the wolves.

                        KING
                       (V.O.)
        Sorry darling, it's too late.

A pack of ravenous wolves enters the arena.

                        PRINCESS
                       (V.O.)
        Oh bother, and I had just fallen in
        love for the first time. Oh spit!

                        QUEEN
             (as in 'language, darling!')
        Good evening!

JAKE backs into a corner with wolves baying and snapping at
his heels. Suddenly, SIR GEORGE is there to save him.

INT. CASTLE. SECRET PASSAGE. DAY

SIR GEORGE pulls JAKE into the narrow, dark chamber. There
is a trapdoor nearby.

                        JAKE
        We did it!

                        SIR GEORGE
        So we did. And your destination is
        there...

He points to the trapdoor. We hear echoing voices drifting
up.

>   MIKE
>   (V.O.)
>   I'd better get off to work...

>   JEAN
>   (V.O.)
>   Shall I make kippers again tomorrow?

JAKE goes to the edge of the trapdoor. He looks back to SIR
GEORGE and speaks with just a trace of regret in his voice.

>   JAKE
>   Is this the end of the adventure?

>   SIR GEORGE
>   The adventure never ends.

He pushes JAKE, who plummets out of sight.

INT. KITCHEN. DAY

JAKE suddenly appears in the kitchen, dressed in his shirt,
blazer and tie. He stands behind a counter. The others are
startled to see him there.

>   MIKE
>   Didn't you — you left for school!

>   JAKE
>   No. Yes. No. You won't believe where I
>   was.

>   JEAN
>   Where were you, dear?

>   JAKE
>   Oh...
>   (he realises the impossibility of
>   explaining)
>   ...out.

MIKE and JEAN exchange looks.

                    SARAH
          You're going to be late for school.

                    JAKE
          I have something to do first.

He walks out. When he comes out from behind the counter we
see he's still got on the page's leotard. Only MIKE catches
a glimpse of this. He frowns but decides he couldn't have
seen what he thought he saw.

INT. JAKE'S ROOM. DAY

JAKE is on his bed, talking into the phone.

                    JAKE
          Hello, is this Elizabeth?... We haven't
          met — my name is Jake Sibley, I've moved
          into the house down the street... You
          have? Yeah, I've seen you, too. Listen,
          I hope this isn't too pushy and American
          of me, but I wondered whether you might
          like to come over after school this
          afternoon...

After a beat, his face breaks into a major smile. As he jabs
his fist into the air in a gesture of victory, we freeze
frame.

FADE OUT

THE END

THE CONCRETE INSPECTOR

When I first approached Graham in the late 1980s with an embryonic story about a man whose job it was to render artistically the cracks in city sidewalks, I half-expected him to tell me to sod off. After all, he was very busy at the time trying to write and get a massive television project (*Jake's Journey*) off the ground. Instead, to my great joy he found the concept amusing enough to contribute many key story ideas and pivotal scenes (for instance, the entire map store scene was his idea). Even though Graham had a general dislike for anything even remotely to do with mime, I think the idea of playing Arthur Privet appealed to him. The fact that Privet was so out of character for him probably appealed to his sense of adventure.

After the initial story was set and key sequences conceived, I took it upon myself to go away and do the actual typing. I would then update Graham as I worked, excising or expounding the script as he felt necessary. The end result was "something completely different" for Graham, which I think pleased him. I know *I* was thrilled.

Any plans for additional stories or even possible productions were quashed by Graham's illness. This script has remained unseen until now.

THE CONCRETE INSPECTOR

By Graham Chapman and Jim Yoakum

©1999 White Bike Productions, Ltd.

VIDEO:

As workmen repair the street we see a burly worker
strenuously mixing and pouring concrete in a big trough. In
the background we hear construction sounds.

>   PRESSMAN
>   (V.O.)
>   Where the hell is Arthur Privet?

>   LAMB
>   (V.O.)
>   White City.

>   PRESSMAN
>   (V.O.)
>   He was supposed to be at Regent Street
>   a half hour ago. There's a two-footer
>   there getting bigger by the minute!

>   LAMB
>   (V.O.)
>   I better get him over there before that
>   bastard blows!

ARTHUR PRIVET is enraptured by the lumpy, liquid concrete
being stirred. He is dressed in khaki shirt and shorts, beige
knee socks and clunky, but highly polished workboots. Perched
on his head is a tin construction hat. He carries wooden
artist's case that folds down into an easel and a bag over
his shoulder. The portable phone that dangles from his
utility belt RINGS and ARTHUR snaps-to. With a little kick
and an elaborate arm gesture he picks it up. (This is how he
always answers the phone.)

>   ARTHUR
>   (into phone)
>   Privet.

>   PRESSMAN
>   (V.O.)
>   Victoria Station. It's a two-footer!

                        ARTHUR
                    (into phone)
              Check chief!

ARTHUR returns the phone and does an about face with a
determined look on his face.

TITLE:
'The Concrete Inspector' is superimposed as we follow ARTHUR
down the street. An upbeat Brazilian tune ('Arthur's Theme')
is heard.

EXT. STREET. DAY

N.B. Arthur has a rather unusual walk, raising and lowering
his legs awkwardly and stiffly, as if they don't fit
properly. He looks like an odd stick insect trying to
extricate itself from some flypaper.

It is very hot. He wipes his brow and eyes a pristine
segment of recently laid sidewalk. He eyes the sun, the
sidewalk. He is concerned. He makes a leaping dive toward
the virgin pavement with the speed and grace of a gazelle.

SLO-MO as ARTHUR flies through the air, his face contorted
in panic. He lands on the sidewalk, spread-eagled. He looks
at the sun and chuckles, pleased with himself for having
saved the sidewalk. Suddenly we hear a CRACKING SOUND.
ARTHUR's face goes slack and he mouths "No!" but the
CRACKING GROWS LOUDER, concluding in a HORRIBLE RIP as the
sidewalk cracks under the hot sun. ARTHUR hangs his head.

EXT. REGENT STREET. DAY

ARTHUR is at the curb. He steps off onto the zebra crossing.
As soon as his foot touches one of the stripes we hear a
PIANO NOTE. ARTHUR is taken aback and he steps off of the
stripe and back onto the curb. After a moment he places
another foot tentatively on a stripe. We hear ANOTHER PIANO
NOTE. He looks around in child-like wonder to see if anyone
else has noticed, but no-one is there. Now getting into it,
he steps on two stripes at once and a PIANO CHORD sounds.
Quite delighted, he jumps and hops from stripe to stripe as
A SERIES OF PIANO NOTES mimic his every step. Satisfied at

last with the fun he moves over to the other side of the curb, dragging his foot, causing a PIANO GLISSANDO. He steps off onto the other curb and continues on. As he moves on we see that there is a piano store on the corner. Off-screen we hear howling laughter.

ARTHUR rounds a corner and stops abruptly, looking down in horror at the pavement. There is a gaping crack in it.

> ARTHUR
> (exclaiming)
> Crumbs!

He shakes at the horrible sight... He approaches the crack and circles it, studying it. Then he gets down on his hands and knees and delicately runs his finger across it. ARTHUR meticulously unfolds his artist's case, turning it into an easel. A MAN stops to watch. ARTHUR concentrates on the crack. He takes a white sketch pad from the case and props it against the easel and, after studying the crack for a moment, opens the brass-studded pouch attached to his belt and extracts a single, charcoal pencil.

A YOUNG COUPLE walks up to see what's going on. The MAN extends his arms protectively, preventing them closer access to ARTHUR.

> MAN
> Watch yourself! Keep clear!

> YOUNG WIFE
> (to MAN)
> What's going on? What's that he's
> doing?

The MAN looks puzzled, unclear as to why he felt compelled to protect ARTHUR.

> MAN
> (to ARTHUR)
> Hey mister, are you doing?

ARTHUR doesn't answer. He continues drawing, concentrating.

An OLDER COUPLE walk up behind the YOUNG COUPLE, to watch.

> OLDER WIFE
> What's going on? Somebody ask him what
> he's doing.

> MAN
> I did ask.

> OLDER WIFE
> Well ask him again! (To ARTHUR)
> Hey mister, what are you doing?

No response from ARTHUR. The MAN taps ARTHUR on the shoulder
and he turns startled to see anyone standing there.

> MAN
> Hey, mister, what are you doing?

> ARTHUR
> (softly, after several elaborate arm gestures)
> It's... technical.

> OLDER WIFE
> What'd he say?

> MAN
> Says it's... technical.

> OLDER WIFE
> What?

> MAN
> Technical.

> OLDER WIFE
> Technical? Well what's that he's
> drawing?

> OLDER HUSBAND
> It looks like he's drawing the cracks
> in the concrete...

The MAN is flustered, he realises that that is <u>exactly</u> what
ARTHUR is doing but he doesn't want to admit it to himself.

                    MAN
                (to OLDER HUSBAND)
        What are you, <u>crazy</u>? You think I'd be
        standing here if... if all he was doing
        was <u>that</u>.
        (Under his breath)
        Crazy old coot...

                OLDER HUSBAND
        Well that's what it looks like to <u>me</u>!

The MANAGER of a nearby store comes out.

                    MANAGER
        Hey, what's going on here?

                    ALL
                (in unison)
        It's technical!

The MANAGER looks at them and then at ARTHUR's drawing.
ARTHUR takes out a complicated-looking measuring device,
gets down on his hands and knees and painstakingly measures
the crack.

                    MANAGER
            Oh.

Satisfied, and totally baffled, he goes back inside his
store. A no-nonsense COP arrives.

                    COP
        Okay, show's over! Everybody go home,
        there's nothing to see here...

Nobody moves. The COP looks at ARTHUR's drawing, pushes his
cap back on his head and scratches his scalp.

                    COP
                (to ARTHUR)
        Are you working for the council?

                        YOUNG HUSBAND
        It's technical.

                            COP
        What?

                            ALL
                        (in unison)
        Technical!

                            COP
        Oh.

The entire group watches ARTHUR for a moment. Then the COP
begins to push the people out of the way.

                            COP
        There's nothing to see here. This is
        all ... technical.

EXT. REGENT STREET. DAY

ARTHUR waits on the corner as SAM SPOONS, enters. He wears
an old-fashioned aviator's cap and goggles and is always
running, out of breath and painfully exhausted. ARTHUR hands
him a rendering and SAM places it into his satchel. He takes
a deep breath then takes off.

EXT. ROOMING HOUSE. DAY

ARTHUR walks up, suitcase in hand. A rotating sprinkler is
watering the lawn. ARTHUR studies it, trying to time his
movements so that he can get to the door without getting
soaked. He makes several false starts, and scurries back to
the gate. Making a mad dash for it, he reaches the front
door without getting wet! He's quite pleased with his
cunning, then he realizes he has dropped his suitcase, which
has landed right in the center of the sprinkler's path.
ARTHUR makes another mad dash for it.

A GARDENER behind some bushes switches off the tap and
unscrews the hose in order to fill a bucket with water.

ARTHUR skids to a stop and picks up his bag. He is relieved

to see that the sprinkler is off and takes his time picking
up his bag.

INT. SITTING ROOM. DAY

MARTINE, a pretty girl, sits at a piano playing a simple
waltz. POPPA, an old man, is playing solitaire and MAMMA, an
old woman, is reading. It is very quiet. We hear the
CREAKING OF A DOOR as it opens and then slams shut. A moment
later we hear the sound of WET SHOES SQUEAKING loudly. We
see ARTHUR tiptoeing toward his room, dripping wet. He stops
and looks at the others then bolts up the stairs to his
room.

INT. ARTHUR'S ROOM/HALLWAY. DAY

Arthur is dressed in boxer shorts and a T-shirt, wringing
out his wet things in the sink. There is a persistent
KNOCKING on the door and he goes to open it. No-one is
there, but sitting outside the door is a small pink cabinet.
He steps out and looks at the cabinet, then down the
hallway, then back at the cabinet, and scratches his head,
confused. MARTINE is now entering her room, directly across
from ARTHUR's. She smiles at him. ARTHUR nods hello and
makes a series of rapid-fire pointing gestures, first at the
cabinet, then at MARTINE and back at the cabinet. He
wriggles his eyebrows quizzically. Is this hers? Is it a
gift from her? MARTINE giggles, enters her room and closes
the door.

A door down the hall CREAKS open an inch and an eye appears
in the crack, watching ARTHUR's every move. ARTHUR looks
over and repeats his rapid-fire series of pointing gestures.
The eye disappears and the door SLAMS shut. ARTHUR shrugs
and stares at the cabinet, hands on hips.

ARTHUR sets the cabinet down on his bed and looks at it from
all angles. He opens his closet door, places the cabinet
inside and shuts the door. He unzips his suitcase and
removes several articles from it: his other inspecting
outfit, an old LP and a small framed drawing of a
particularly spectacular crack.

He places the framed drawing on his dresser and then
carefully removes a child's drawing of a girl from his case
and, with a sentimental smile, starts to tape it to the
wall. He spies a crack in the wall and delicately runs his
finger over it, then he tapes the drawing next to it. He
spies a brochure on top of the dresser and picks it up.

The brochure reads

        'Good Food Fast! Just a Tube Stop from YOU!'

INT. TRAIN CAR. DAY

A crowded car. ARTHUR sits by the window, happily
anticipating his good food. ARTHUR's attention is grabbed by
a group of HINDU PEOPLE who are sitting across from him.
They are speaking very fast and all at the same time. Each
person is also speaking at a slightly different pitch and,
as ARTHUR concentrates on their staccato dialogue, their
voices change. IN ARTHUR'S MIND they become like the CALLS
OF SEAGULLS, SCREAMING and SCREECHING. He closes his eyes
and shakes his head several times racked in pain and agony.
Will the noise ever stop? His vision goes fuzzy... A moment
later and everything is back to normal. ARTHUR sighs,
exhausted.

EXT. TUBE STATION. DAY

The train pulls into a station. Several people exit, and
just as many take their place.

INT. TRAIN CAR. DAY

Arthur looks out the window, into the car of the train on
the other side of the tracks and does a double-take. Inside
the car is a middle-aged housewife, dressed in a dowdy
bathrobe, her hair in curlers. Under her arm she carries a
bag of groceries. This is 'THE WOMAN'. She spots ARTHUR and
her eyes light up.

                        THE WOMAN
            Yoo hoo! Monsieur! Excuse me, Monsieur!

She waves a white handkerchief, rises from her seat, never

taking her eyes off of Arthur, and exits her car.

ARTHUR is scared to death. He squirms in his seat as panic sets in. He tries to get up but the car is too crowded. Suddenly THE WOMAN appears outside ARTHUR's window. She pounds on the glass and waves the hanky. He is in a panic.

                    THE WOMAN
          Monsieur, please!

The train jerks to life and starts to chug out of the station. THE WOMAN trots alongside the car, pounding and pleading.

EXT. ARTHUR'S TRAIN WINDOW. DAY

CLOSE-UP on ARTHUR as he presses his nose against the window watching THE WOMAN. She stops at the edge of the platform and shouts after him. His face is a portrait in bug-eyed panic.

FADE TO BLACK

INT. ARTHUR'S SHOWER. DAY

Arthur is covered head to toe in soap. He is singing along to his stereo, enjoying himself immensely. Suddenly we hear an INTENSE BANGING and SCUFFLING. ARTHUR stops and listens. Silence. He resumes bathing. A moment later MORE PROLONGED BANGING. ARTHUR ignores it and finishes bathing. He switches off the water, wraps a large Turkish towel around himself.

INT. ARTHUR'S BEDROOM. DAY

ARTHUR stops and stares in disbelief. The pink cabinet is sitting in the middle of his bed. His closet door is swinging slowly on its hinges. His portable phone RINGS. With a little kick and elaborate arm gesture, he picks it up.

                    ARTHUR
                  (into phone)
          Privet.

                              PRESSMAN
                         (V.O. desperately)
                     Keats Grove. It's a yawner!

                              ARTHUR
                         (into phone)
                I'm on it!

He exits.

INT. ARTHUR'S BEDROOM. DAY (LATER)

ARTHUR is not in the room. There is a KNOCK on the door.
After a moment it CREAKS open and MOMMA sticks her head in
then enters with a dust mop and a bucket. She sees the pink
cabinet on the bed and mutters under her breath as she picks
it up and carries it out of the room.

EXT. STREET. DAY

ARTHUR walking down the street, trailed by a pack of dogs.
After a moment he stops and looks at the bottom of his shoe.
He frowns and shakes a reproaching finger at the dogs. Then
he sighs, pats a dog on the head and continues on his way,
dragging the sole of his shoe along the pavement as he goes.
He comes to the corner and stops.

CLOSE-UP on crossing light. ARTHUR can't cross. After a
moment he begins to whistle 'Arthur's Theme'. A BANKER
ambles up behind him and stops, waiting to cross. After a
moment he too begins to whistle quietly along with the tune.
ARTHUR is oblivious. They are joined by TWO HIPSTERS who
stop, wait. Soon they too are whistling and humming along
with ARTHUR.

After a moment a small group of TOURISTS stop, wait and soon
sing along. Slowly they grow in confidence, their voices get
louder. Those that won't sing are bullied into it and the
odd fight breaks out. ARTHUR watches the light. The
MOTORISTS who are waiting at the light begin to sing along,
as do OFFICE WORKERS who hang out their windows.

CLOSE-UP on crossing light. It changes and ARTHUR cautiously
looks both ways, even though all traffic is stopped and

everyone is singing and fighting. ARTHUR makes his way down the next block. He comes to the corner and stops.

CLOSE-UP on crossing light. ARTHUR can't cross. He waits for the light to change. A moment later he is joined by a STERN-FACED ACCOUNTANT. ARTHUR smiles to himself and begins to whistle 'Arthur's Theme' to himself.

EXT. CITY STREET. DAY

ARTHUR sees a sign in the window of a short two-story building. It reads: 'Maps For Sale'. He enters.

INT. BUILDING. DAY

ARTHUR is staring at the building directory. It lists nine floors:
Basement: dirty diapers, iron lungs, tree stumps, gravel.
Ground Floor: calibrated motors, celebrity autographs, gossip, hair salon, maps.
Mezzanine Level: planks, rubber tubing, castrations, bottled beers, electric calendars.
First floor: pre-chewed food, pressurised cleaning, mirrors, compliments, back injuries.
Second Floor: poems, leaf blowers, spare tyres, spared rods, spoiled food, soiled linen, nasty things, carts and horses.
Third Floor: mezzanine.
Fourth Floor: swimming pool, sauna, oral sex.
Fifth Floor: bandages, hair bonnets, toupees, vivisections.
Sixth Floor: certain death.

ARTHUR looks puzzled, turns and exits.

EXT. BUILDING. DAY

ARTHUR stops and looks up at the building. It only has two floors. He shrugs and re-enters the building.

INT. BUILDING. DAY

ARTHUR walks over to the elevator and presses The 'up' button. The doors open. An ELEVATOR OPERATOR, an old man in a posh uniform, is inside. ARTHUR gets in.

INT. ELEVATOR. DAY

ARTHUR looks at the button panel. It has twelve buttons. He
gives the ELEVATOR OPERATOR an odd look. The ELEVATOR
OPERATOR stares blankly at ARTHUR.

                    ELEVATOR OPERATOR
                    (as the doors shut)
          Floor please.

INT. SECOND FLOOR. DAY.

The elevator doors open and ARTHUR exits with a tumble. He
sees the map store and enters.

INT. MAP STORE. DAY

All this store sells is maps and globes.

The STORE OWNER is on the telephone.

                    STORE OWNER
                    (on phone)
          I didn't say that. No I'm not arguing
          with you. I didn't say that. That's not
          what I said. No I'm not arguing with
          you...

The STORE OWNER points out the self-serve map aisle to
ARTHUR. Out of curiosity ARTHUR picks up a folded map and
begins to unfurl it. It keeps unfolding. After a moment it
must be six feet square and there's still more inside. He
begins to panic and refold the map. He places it back on the
rack.

CLOSE-UP on map. It reads: 'World Map. Actual Size'.

ARTHUR finds the correct map of the city and moves to the
register to pay for it.

EXT. TAXI STAND. DAY

ARTHUR pulls the map out of his pocket and glances at it as

he hails a taxi. As the cab pulls up, we hear an ALARM go off. ARTHUR turns to see what the commotion is about. A BANK ROBBER scurries past and a bundle of hundreds falls to the pavement. ARTHUR picks it up and hands it back to the BANK ROBBER. A HARRIED BUSINESS WOMAN enters and grabs his cab when he's not looking and pulls away. A second car pulls up. ARTHUR opens the door and gets in, thinking it's his cab.

INT. TAXI. DAY

Before ARTHUR can tell the cabby the address, the BANK ROBBER also pushes his way inside and the car peels out. The car is obviously the getaway car and before they go a hundred yards the police fall in behind them.

EXT. STREETS. DAY

The crooks' car skids around a corner followed quickly by the zebra car.

INT. TAXI. DAY

Arthur leans forward and shows his map to the DRIVER, indicating where he needs to go. The BANK ROBBER and the DRIVER glare at him suspiciously. We hear GUNFIRE from the police car and a LOUD BANG. The tyres of the crooks' car have been hit by the cops and the car begins to swerve violently. The DRIVER can't control the car.

EXT. STREETS. DAY

O.S. We hear a TERRIBLE SKIDDING OF TYRES followed by a LOUD CAR CRASH and then the HISSING OF THE RADIATOR. After a moment a lone hubcap rolls across the frame. A moment after that ARTHUR enters, dusting himself off. A street sign catches attention.

CLOSE-UP on street sign. It reads 'Keats Grove'.

ARTHUR turns and tips his hat to the robbers, then promptly heads off toward the street.

EXT. KEAT'S GROVE. DAY

Arthur immediately begins to search for 'the yawner'. As
before, he raises his legs and lunges forward as he points
at the crack accusingly, an impish grin on his face, pleased
at finding his prey.

                        ARTHUR
          Ah-ha!

He drops to the pavement and approaches the crack on his
hands and knees.

          Easy big fella...

He whips out his portable phone and dials.

          I'm going in.

                        PRESSMAN
                        (V.O.)
          God be with you, Arthur Privet...

ARTHUR delicately runs his finger up and down the crack. A
whispery female voice speaks from out of the crack.

                        PAMPLINA
                        (V.O.)
          No.

Startled, Arthur pulls his finger away and peers into the
crack. He looks to see if anyone is looking as he presses
his lips close to it.

                        ARTHUR
          Hello?

                        PAMPLINA
                        (V.O.)
          I'm Pamplina.

                        ARTHUR
          I'm...

> PAMPLINA
> (V.O.)
> I know who you are. I've been waiting
> for you.

> ARTHUR
> (puzzled)
> Why?

> PAMPLINA
> (V.O.)
> Shhh! Somebody's coming.

SAM SPOONS enters running in place, exhausted as usual.

> ARTHUR
> Pamplina.
> (Points at crack)
> In the yawner.

CLOSE-UP on crack. It's gone.

INT. SITTING ROOM/ROOMING HOUSE. DAY

A series of CLOSE-UPS of ordinary objects in the room. We
hear a beautiful classical piano piece playing.

> FEMALE
> (V.O.)
> I just love this music. The pianist
> plays it with such passion...

> MALE
> (V.O.)
> Just listen to the tonalities! Such a
> delicate touch...

> FEMALE
> (V.O.)
> It's awe-inspiring.

> MALE
> (V.O.)
> More wine?

We hear THE SOUND OF WINE BEING POURED.

> FEMALE
> (V.O.)
> Such a diverse range of styles...We are
> listening to a musical genius.

> MALE
> (V.O.)
> More than genius, it's almost as if God
> himself were speaking through this
> music!

> FEMALE
> (V.O.)
> Listen... listen to this passage...you
> can almost see the babbling brook and
> the way the sun glistens off the dew-
> dappled leaves.

> MALE
> (V.O.)
> More cheese?

CLOSE-UP on cassette deck. The cassette tape reaches the end
of the side and CLICKS OFF. The music stops, as do the
voices. After a moment a male hand enters the shot, ejects
the tape, flips it over and presses the 'play' button. After
a moment a different PIANO PIECE and the voices, begin.

> MALE
> (V.O.)
> This piece is spellbinding. What a rare
> talent.

> FEMALE
> (V.O.)
> The richness is overwhelming...

As the voices continue we SLOWLY PULL BACK TO REVEAL ARTHUR
sitting alone at the piano. He is playing the piano music we
are listening to. He is all alone in the room.

INT. SITTING ROOM/BOARDING HOUSE. NIGHT

ARTHUR is sitting with MARTINE, POPPA and MOMMA, eating
supper. Everyone but ARTHUR eats from a tray. He balances
his plate on his knees. The room is very quiet. We hear the
muffled ticking of a clock. ARTHUR cuts his food into many
tiny bites and then eats each bite separately, chewing
thoroughly and swallowing it completely, before spearing the
next one. After every bite he looks up at the others and
smiles. MARTINE smiles back, warmly. POPPA speaks suddenly,
alarming ARTHUR.

                    POPPA
                 (to Arthur)
          So, what do you do Mr Privet?

                    ARTHUR
            (after a prolonged chewing bout)
          Concrete inspector.

                    POPPA
          What'd he say, momma?

                    MOMMA
          Said he's a concert conductor.

                    POPPA
          What the bloody hell is _that_?

                    ARTHUR
        (waving fork around, searching for right word)
             It's... _technical_.

                    POPPA
          What'd he say?

                    MARTINE
          He said it's _technical_ poppa.

ARTHUR smiles and nods to everyone as he continues eating.

                    POPPA
          Technical huh? Then I bet he worked on
          the new by-pass.

                    MARTINE
          Ooh, that's a good one!

                    POPPA
                 (with gravity)
          Cuts travel time to Bridgewater by
          eight point three minutes.

                    MOMMA
          I'm not sure I like the idea of renting
          out to musicians...

                    POPPA
          Course your technical's alright, but it
          don't feed the bulldog! Now me, I'm a
          self-made man.

                    MARTINE
          Oh Poppa...

                    POPPA
     (holds his hands up and looks at them, wistfully)
          Bands of steel...
          (suddenly hard)
          Let's see your technical do that!

He pounds his hands down on his tray in defiance and glares
at ARTHUR who looks at POPPA and nods his head, smiling and
chewing.

                    MOMMA
          Jenny's boy was a musician. Used to
          pull a rabbit out of a hat.

MARTINE looks shyly at ARTHUR giggles and looks away.

INT. SITTING ROOM. NIGHT — LATER

The mood is festive. POPPA stands beside a gramophone
clapping enthusiastically as a ridiculous rendition of
'Turkey In The Straw' plays. ARTHUR and the two women
dancing wildly. ARTHUR executes a particularly impressive
kick-spin and the two women stop dancing and join in the
clapping, egging him on.

Suddenly the record starts skipping and, thrown off of the
rhythm, the two women stop clapping and watch as ARTHUR
maniacally repeats his kick-spin in perfect sync with the
skip.

INT. ARTHUR'S ROOM/HALLWAY. NIGHT

ARTHUR is dressed in his underwear. He is trying to make
coffee. He takes a fresh filter down and puts it into the Mr
Coffee. Then he takes down the coffee can and pours it into
the filter — but the can is empty. He looks down at the
wastebasket and opens the lid. Inside is yesterday's coffee
filter. He picks it up and dumps the used grounds into the
fresh filter, pours in the water and continues to make
morning coffee.

We hear a faint RAPPING in the distance. A bit startled,
ARTHUR puts his ear to the coffee pot and listens. The
rapping has stopped. He goes back to preparing coffee. More
RAPPING. ARTHUR puts his hand on his hip and looks around
the room as if to say 'Okay, what's going on?' We hear the
RAPPING SOUND AGAIN, LOUDER. ARTHUR begins to search for the
cause of it. With each RAP he sets off in a different
direction, ultimately going out the door.

ARTHUR steps into the hallway, looking up and down. At the
far end is a single, closed door. The mysterious rapping
leads him slowly towards it. He cranes his ear along the
floor and up the wall, attempting to find where the rapping
is coming from. He stops at the door. The RAPPING CONTINUES
ERRATICALLY. ARTHUR slowly opens the door. It CREAKS LOUDLY.
He flips on the light switch quickly and freezes. There,
halfway up the basement stairs sits the pink cabinet!

                    ARTHUR
                   (loudly)
          Ha!

ARTHUR sternly and dramatically points at the pink cabinet,
staring it down, daring it to move. A large box falls on his
head, he goes limp and falls to the ground like a spent
puppet.

MIX THROUGH TO ARTHUR on a chaise lounge. He jerks awake, shaking himself at finding himself in a beautiful garden, with the sun shining and birds singing. His MOTHER is pouring him a jug of iced fruit juice, gently nudging him awake.

> MOTHER
>
> Come on dear...

> ARTHUR
>
> Mother!

> MOTHER
>
> Wake up dear.

> ARTHUR
>
> So, it was all a dream.

> MOTHER
>
> No dear, this is the dream. You're still at the horrible, smelly old boarding house.

INT. HALLWAY. NIGHT

ARTHUR wakes up on the floor, staring blankly into space.

CLOSE-UP on a starry night.

It looks to be a cool, crisp evening. The stars are twinkling and the sky is as black as ink. We hear the CHIRPING OF CRICKETS. Suddenly there is the RINGING of a telephone.

> ARTHUR
> (into phone)
>
> Privet.

> PRESSMAN
> (voice over)
>
> Dorking.

A hand enters the shot and appears to actually grab hold of the night sky and seemingly peel back a section of it. Behind the sky we see a window and through this window we see incredibly bright sunshine and a city street.

PULL BACK TO REVEAL:

INT. ARTHUR'S ROOM/BOARDING HOUSE. MORNING

We now realise that we are ARTHUR's bedroom, and that his window has been covered with a piece of cloth decorated with glow-in-the dark stars. ARTHUR sits up in bed dressed in his underwear. He removes the cloth, rolls it up and peers out the window.

INT. COACH. DAY

ARTHUR is boarding the coach. It is very crowded and he has to squeeze himself into the seat of a VERY FAT MAN in order to have a place to sit. He looks out the window, excited about his journey. Suddenly he gets a startled look in his eyes. Through the window we see a figure running toward the bus. It gets closer and we see that it's THE WOMAN still dressed as before.

> THE WOMAN
> (waving the hanky)
> Monsieur! Please wait!

CLOSE-UP on ARTHUR. He is in a panic. He stands up, changes his mind and sits, changes his mind and stands then sits. Just as THE WOMAN gets within feet of the bus it jerks to a start and pulls out.

EXT. BUS WINDOW. DAY

CLOSE-UP on ARTHUR'S FACE pressed against the window. He watches THE WOMAN as she stands on the sidewalk waving and calling after him. The bus merges with the traffic. Among the many cars on the road is a small lorry loaded down with boxes, lamps, chairs — and a pink cabinet.

FADE OUT

THE END

TONIGHT: VD

This never-before seen short piece was 'a sketch in progress' and was written by Graham in the late 1980s. It is an excellent example of Graham's complete bewilderment at society's seeming inability to confront normal human things (like disease) in a rational, sensible and adult manner. "Why *can't* we use words like 'cancer'?" he once pondered after the BBC had edited a *Monty Python* sketch in which they removed the word 'cancer' and inserted the word 'gangrene' instead. "A lot of people die of cancer and if more people spoke about it more openly then perhaps more of them would be cured. It's silly to be afraid of things like cancer and hide things away." Typically, after the refreshingly candid star died of throat cancer in 1989, idiotic rumours began to spread that he had actually died from AIDS but had been afraid to admit he had the disease.

Graham's good humour under trying circumstances is maybe best summed up in this telling anecdote by his long-time companion, David Sherlock, "After Graham's second cancer operation on his spine he was at a recording for a *Python* TV special. At this time he was completely paralysed from the waist down and was in a wheelchair. As we crossed the floor at Twickenham Studios, negotiating cables and cameras, a technician that Graham had known for years called across to him, 'Hi Graham, how you doing?' he said. 'Fine', replied Graham, 'it's just this fucking cancer that's the problem!'"

The original manuscript of this sketch features several doodles along the top of the page which, according to David Sherlock, indicates that it was written in Graham's post-boozing days: "Otherwise it'd have had gin and tonic stains all over it!"

TONIGHT: VD

By Graham Chapman 1988

> CHAPMAN
> (V.O.)
> Good evening. Tonight, VD, an ever-increasing
> social menace, a problem which rears its
> ugly head in front of innocent adults and
> teenagers alike — innocent because of their
> lack of knowledge of this easily eradicable
> group of diseases — diseases which, if
> public had more knowledge, would disappear
> forever. Why isn't there more education in
> schools, most particularly about VD? Why is
> there a conspiracy of silence about even
> mentioning this important and easily
> eradicable plague on society? Why should even
> the mention of those ominous letters 'VD',
> reduce society to an ignorant silence? There
> is no shame in contracting VD. No more than
> catching a common cold. You should be able
> to go along to your doctor or hospital, just
> as with a cold in the nose and say "I have a
> cold in the dong". It's only a disease after
> all, not a moral issue, and it can be cured.
> Good God! I mean, Great Heavens! By Jove!
> Must we all be so juvenile? It's only two
> letters for God's sake...

As the lecturer continues his rather sensible talk on VD, we
overhear the voices of two television controllers.

> CONTROLLER #1
> Cut him off.

> CONTROLLER #2
> Why?

> CONTROLLER #1
> He said 'dong'

> CONTROLLER #2
> What do you mean, 'dong'?

> CONTROLLER #1
> Well, er, <u>thing</u>, er, between the, er...

> CONTROLLER #2
>
> What?

> CONTROLLER #1
>
> Well... legs.

> CONTROLLER #2
>
> Legs? He didn't say legs.

> CONTROLLER #1
>
> No. 'Dong'.

> CONTROLLER #2
>
> What's that?

> CONTROLLER #1
>
> Well, er, you know. Er, a, erm, sort of,
> well... we've all got one. Erm, except my
> wife, of course. She has... er... women
> have... well, men have, umm... you know:
> willies!

> CONTROLLER #2
>
> He didn't say 'willies'! My God, cut him
> off!

> CONTROLLER #1
>
> Cut off his willie?

> CONTROLLER #2
>
> No, you fool, axe the programme!

> CONTROLLER #1
>
> Oh, axe the programme! Right.

> CHAPMAN
> [V.O.]
>
> ...I mean, 'penis' or 'willie', there are
> many names for it. Younger listeners might
> say 'willie' for instance...

He is cut off

THE END

A SELECTED CHAPMANOGRAPHY

GRAHAM CHAPMAN BOOKS

THE ODD JOB
by Bernard McKenna and Colin Bostock-Smith

(the novelisation of the film that was co-written, co-produced by, and starred Graham Chapman; it is about an English gentleman who becomes depressed when his wife leaves him and hires an odd job man to help him commit suicide)

- Arrow Books, 1978 (UK)
  ISBN 0-09-918950-X (paperback)

———

A LIAR'S AUTOBIOGRAPHY, VOL. VI
by Graham Chapman

(an autobiography by Graham Chapman; Chapman begins with lengthier fantasy passages and eases into his own real-life story; he discusses frankly his battle with alcohol, his homosexuality, his medical studies and his involvement with Python; written contributions were also provided by David Sherlock, Alex Martin, David Yallop and Douglas Adams; it is also available on audio cassette)

- Eyre Methuen, Ltd., 1980 (UK)
  ISBN 0-413-47570-0 (hardcover)
- Magnum Books/Eyre Methuen, 1981 (UK)
  ISBN 0-417-07200-7 (paperback)
- Methuen London, Ltd., 1984 (UK)
  ISBN 0-417-07200-7 (paperback)
- Methuen, 1980 (US) ISBN 0-416-00901-8 (hardcover)
- Mandarin, 1991 ISBN 0-7493-0817-6 (paperback)

———

THE SECRET POLICEMAN'S OTHER BALL

(book contains scripts and photos, with programme notes throughout by Terry Jones and Michael Palin, book includes an 'Introduction' by John Cleese and the cast; also starred Graham Chapman)

- Methuen, 1981 (UK) ISBN 0-413-50080-2 (paperback)

FOOTLIGHTS!: A HUNDRED YEARS OF CAMBRIDGE COMEDY (1983)

- Methuen, 1983 (UK) ISBN 0-413-56050-3 (paperback)

———

YELLOWBEARD
by Graham Chapman and David Sherlock

(based on the screenplay by Graham Chapman, Peter Cook and Bernard McKenna; the story of Yellowbeard, a notorious pirate, who escapes from prison and goes in search of his son and his buried treasure; 64 pages)

- Sphere, 1983 (UK) ISBN 0-7221-2347-7

———

THE GOLDEN SKITS OF WING COMMANDER MURIEL VOLESTRANGLER FRHS & BAR
by John Cleese (with Graham Chapman, Tim Brooke-Taylor, Marty Feldman and many others)

- Methuen, 1984 (UK) ISBN 0-413-41560-0 (paperback)

———

THE COURAGE TO CHANGE: HOPE AND HELP FOR ALCOHOLICS AND THEIR FAMILIES
by Dennis Wholey

(a collection of interviews with well-known alcoholics and their families, in which they discuss their battles with alcohol; included is a chapter on Graham Chapman)

• Houghten Mifflin, 1984 (US)
ISBN 0-395-35977-5 (paperback)
• Warner Books, 1986 (US)
ISBN 0-446-35758-8 (paperback)

———

THE UTTERLY, UTTERLY MERRY COMIC RELIEF CHRISTMAS BOOK
(contains material by Michael Palin, Terry Jones, and Graham Chapman)

• Fontana Trade Paperback, 1986 (UK)
ISBN 0-00-637-128-0

———

GRAHAM CRACKERS: FUZZY MEMORIES, SILLYBITS AND OUTRIGHT LIES
by Graham Chapman
(compiled by Jim Yoakum)

(a semi-sequel to Graham Chapman's A Liar's Autobiography. Contains a Foreword by John Cleese, a Backword by Eric Idle and a Sideways by Terry Jones)

• The Career Press, 1997 (US) ISBN 1-56414-334-1

———

OJRIL: THE COMPLETELY INCOMPLETE GRAHAM CHAPMAN
by Graham Chapman with Douglas Adams, David Sherlock and Jim Yoakum (edited by Jim Yoakum for the Graham Chapman Archives)

(a collection of never-published and [hardly-ever] produced scripts including Jake's Journey *and* Our Show for Ringo Starr*)*

• BT Batsford, 1999 (UK)
ISBN 0-7134-8605-8

———

GRAHAM CHAPMAN RECORDINGS

LP = Long Playing Record Album | SI = Single |
CS = Cassette Tape | CD = Compact Disc

THE FROST REPORT ON BRITAIN (1966)

(produced by James Gilbert; writing credits: David Frost and John Cleese, with Tim Brooke-Taylor, Graham Chapman, Barry Cryer, Tony Hendra, Terry Jones, Herbert Kretzner, Peter Lewis and Peter Dobereiner, David Nobbs, Bill Oddie and Ludwig Van Beethoven)

SIDE ONE: Matter of Taste; Schoolmaster; Just Four Just Men; Internal Combustion; Deck of Cards; Top of the Form; Unknown Soldier

SIDE TWO: Scrapbook; Adventure; Numbers; Bulletin; Hilton; Zookeeper

- LP: (1966) Parlophone PMC 7005 (UK)
- LP: (1966) EMI Records-Starline MRS 5084 (UK)

———

THE FROST REPORT ON EVERYTHING (1967)

(Features David Frost, Ronnie Barker, John Cleese, Ronnie Corbett and Sheila Steafel; writing credits include Frost, Terry Jones, Michael Palin, Eric Idle, Graham Chapman and John Cleese [mis-spelled 'Clease'])

SIDE ONE: The State of England; Theatre Critic; Frost, What People Really Mean; Three Classes of People; Narcissus Complex

SIDE TWO: Frost on Agriculture, Speech; The Secretary; Frost on Commercials; Selling String; Executive and the Teaman; Three Classes

- LP: (1967) Janus JLS-3005 (UK)

———

A POKE IN THE EYE (WITH A SHARP STICK) (1976)

(recording of the 1976 Amnesty International Benefit; features John Cleese, Graham Chapman, Terry Gilliam, Terry Jones, Michael Palin, Carol Cleveland, Neil Innes, Alan Bennett, John Bird, Eleanor Bron, Tim Brooke-Taylor, Peter Cook, John Fortune, Jonathan Miller, Jonathan Lynn, Graeme Garden, Bill Oddie)

SIDE ONE: A Brief Introduction (Cleese); Asp (Cook, Fortune); Happy, Darling? (Bron, Fortune); The Last Supper (Cleese, Lynn); Telegram (Bennett); Funky Gibbon (The Goodies—Brooke-Taylor, Garden, Oddie); Appeal (Bron)

SIDE TWO: Courtroom (Chapman, Cleese, Cleveland, Gilliam, Jones, Palin, with Cook); Portraits from Memory (Miller); You Say Potato (Bird, Fortune); Baby Talk (Bron, Fortunc); So That's The Way You Like It — Beyond the Fringe (Miller, Bennett, Cook with Jones); Lumberjack Song (All)

- LP: (1976) Transatlantic/TRA 331 (UK)

———

THE SECRET POLICEMAN'S OTHER BALL (1981)

(the 1981 Amnesty International Comedy Gala recorded at the Theatre Royal, Drury Lane, London on September 9 through 12, 1981; featuring: John Cleese, Graham Chapman, Neil Innes, John Bird, Rowan Atkinson, Jasper Carrott, Pamela Stephenson, Victoria Wood, John Fortune, Alan Bennett, Alexei Sayle, Dame Edna Everage, John Wells, Griff Rhys Jones, Chris Langham, Tim Brooke-Taylor, Billy Connolly)

SIDE ONE: A Word of Thanks (Cleese and the cast); Road Safety (Atkinson); Australian Motor Insurance Claims (Carrott); Clothes Off (Cleese, Stephenson, Chapman); Had it Up to Here (Wood), Men's Talk (Fortune, Bennett), What's On In Stoke Newington (Sayle)

SIDE TWO: The Royal Australian Prostate Foundation (Everage); Denis on the Menace (Wells); Beekeeping (Cleese, Atkinson); Song in a French Accent (Innes): Divorce Service (Atkinson, Rhys Jones, Stephenson, Fortune); Reading the Riot Act (Langham); Top of the Form (Cleese, Chapman, Brooke-Taylor, Bird, Rhys Jones, Fortune, Atkinson); Drinking (Connolly)

- LP: (1981) Springtime (also cited as being published by Island), HAHA 6003 (UK)

———

COMIC RELIEF: UTTERLY UTTERLY LIVE! (1986)

(Stephen Fry, Bob Geldof, and Midge Ure perform Merchant Banker *originally written by John Cleese and Graham Chapman)*

- LP: (1986) WEA Records / 24 09321 (UK)

———

A LIAR'S AUTOBIOGRAPHY (1989)

(Graham Chapman reads from his own autobiography, two cassette tapes, unabridged 182 minutes; distributed by Dove Books on Tape, Inc.; in the US call 1-800-345-9945)

- CS: (1989) Dove Books on Tape, Inc., ISBN 1-55800-120-4 (US)

———

A POKE IN THE EYE (WITH A SHARP STICK), VOL. II also called THE COMPLETE A POKE IN THE EYE (WITH A SHARP STICK) (1991)

(1991 reissue of the original 1976 album, features a full bonus album of material not included on the original album)

- LP: (1991) A POKE IN THE EYE (WITH A SHARP STICK), VOL. II, Castle Communications ESD 153 (UK)
- CD: (1991) THE COMPLETE A POKE IN THE EYE (WITH A SHARP STICK) Castle Communications ESDCD 153 (UK)

———

THE COMPLETE SECRET POLICEMAN'S OTHER BALL (1991)

- CD: (1991) Castle Communications ESDCD 152 (UK)

———

THE SECRET POLICEMAN'S OTHER BALL: THE MUSIC (1992)

(this is the tenth anniversary reissue of the 1982 album; the album includes John Cleese introducing Jeff Beck and Eric Clapton; liner notes include a history of the Amnesty International galas with pictures of John Cleese and Graham Chapman; music performers on this album include: Sting, Jeff Beck, Eric Clapton, Bob Geldof, Phil Collins, Donovan, and the star-studded Secret Police)

- CD: (1992) Rhino / Springtime R2 71048 (US)

———

DEAD PARROT SOCIETY: THE BEST OF BRITISH COMEDY (1993)

(includes material from A Poke in the Eye (With a Sharp Stick), A Poke in the Eye (With a Sharp Stick), Vol. II, *and* The Secret Policeman's Other Ball*)*

TRACK LISTING: Also Sprach Zarathustra; The Dead Parrot (Monty Python); The Courtroom-Scene I: *The Charges* (Monty Python); Memoirs of a Miner — Part I; Protest Song (Neil Innes); Happy, Darling?; The Courtroom-Scene II: *Counsel for the Defence* (Monty Python); Psychedelic Baby; Crunchy Frog (Monty Python); Memoirs of a Miner-Part II; The Oral Majority!-Part I (Graham Chapman);

The William Tell Overture; The Courtroom-Scene III: *Police Constable Pan Am* (Monty Python); The Audition; Top of the Form (John Cleese, Graham Chapman, and company); Transcendental Mastication; The Courtroom-Scene IV: *Counsel for the Prosecution* (Monty Python); Overture/Pinball Wizard (Live!); The Penultimate Supper?! (John Cleese, Jonathan Lynn); Take of Your Clothes!; The Courtroom-Scene V: *Very Expensive Gaiters* (Monty Python); Memoirs of a Miner-Part III; The Oral Majority-Part II (Graham Chapman); Balls!; The Courtroom-Scene VI: *There Goes the Judge* (Monty Python); The Argument Clinic (Monty Python); Classical Massacre!; The Lumberjack Song (Monty Python and cast)

• CD: (1993) Rhino Records R2 71049 (US)

———

A SIX PACK OF LIES (1997)

(Graham Chapman live on stage)

TRACK LISTING: 30 Seconds of Abuse, The Dangerous Sports Club, Shitties, The Even More Dangerous Keith Moon, Monty Python's Fliegende Zirkus, Two Films and Six Snakes, Paralysed at the Polo Lounge, The (Non-Inflatable) History of Monty Python, Who Wrote What (And Who Didn't), A Horse, A Bucket and a Spoon?, Python's Progress (circa 1988), And Then There Was...Spam!!!, The Magic Christian, A Liar's Autobiography

• CD: (1997) Verbatim Records CDVB 001 (UK)

———

GRAHAM CHAPMAN VIDEOS

HOW TO IRRITATE PEOPLE (1968)

• Castle Communications, under licence from David Paradine Productions, distributed by White Star (1995) VHS 1656 (ISBN 1-56127-656-1), 65 mins

———

THE MAGIC CHRISTIAN (1969)

(from the novel by Terry Southern; additional material by John Cleese and Graham Chapman; story is about the richest man in the world, Sir Guy Grand *played by Peter Sellers, who adopts a dishevelled young man,* Youngman Grand *played by Ringo Starr; includes appearances by John Cleese as a* Director in Sotheby's *and Graham Chapman as an* Oxford Team Member)

• Grand Films Ltd., distributed by Republic Pictures Home Video (1991), VHS 2548 (ISBN 1-55526-347-X), 101 mins (actually closer to 93 mins)

———

DOCTOR IN TROUBLE (1970)

(seventh feature film based on the book Doctor in the House; *featured Graham Chapman as* Roddy; *Graham Chapman and John Cleese also wrote and co-wrote a number of television episodes starting in 1969 for London Weekend Television's* Doctor in the House *series)*

• Rank Films, distributed by Rank (UK), VC3458, 90 mins

———

RENTADICK (1972)

(film about a detective agency, Rentadick, Inc., that is hired to find a stolen nerve gas that paralyses its victims from the waist down; written by John Cleese and Graham Chapman; disagreements about the production of this film led Cleese and Chapman to disassociate themselves with it)

• Rank Films/Paradine-Virgin, distributed by Rank, 94 mins

———

THE ODD JOB (1978)

(starring Graham Chapman, screenplay and production also by Graham Chapman; Chapman plays the role of Arthur Harris, *an English gentleman who becomes depressed when his wife leaves him and hires an odd job man to help him commit suicide)*

• Columbia Pictures, presented by Atlantic Television, Inc./Charisma Films, distributed by Vestron Video (1984), VA 4120, 86 mins

———

SHOCK TREATMENT (has also been cited as TRAITEMENT DE CHOC) (1981)

(little known fact about a little known film; Graham Chapman and David Sherlock acted as uncredited advisors on this semi-sequel to the 1975 cult classic, The Rocky Horror Picture Show; *Brad and Janet, now married and portrayed by different leads, find themselves trapped on a TV gameshow full of weirdoes)*

• distributed by CBS/Fox Home Video (US), TWT 1184, 94 mins

———

THE SECRET POLICEMAN'S OTHER BALL (1982)

(highlights from the first two Amnesty International Balls; with Graham Chapman, John Cleese, Terry Jones and Michael Palin)

- Miramax Films, distributed by MGM/UA Home Video / Miramax Films, MV800175, 101 mins
- Miramax Films, distributed by Columbia Tristar Home Video (UK), CVR21432, 101 mins
- Miramax Films, distributed by Sony Music Operations / Columbia Tristar Home Video (UK), CVR 16917, 92 mins

———

YELLOWBEARD (1983)

(written by Graham Chapman, Peter Cook and Bernard McKenna; featuring Graham Chapman as Yellowbeard, John Cleese as Blind Pew and Eric Idle as Commander Clement; story of Yellowbeard, a notorious pirate, who escapes from prison and goes in search of his son and his buried treasure)

- Hemdale Films / Orion Pictures, distributed by Video Treasures, SV 9138, 97 mins
- Hemdale Films / Orion Pictures, distributed by Vestron Video (1983), VES 5024 (has also been cited as VA 5024), 97 mins
- Hemdale Films / Orion Pictures, distributed by Orion Home Video (1996), 8304 (ISBN 1-56255-247-3), 97 mins

———

GROUP MADNESS: THE MAKING OF YELLOWBEARD (1983)

(behind the scenes footage of the making of Yellowbeard with Graham Chapman, John Cleese, Eric Idle and others; includes interviews with most of the cast; this film had a limited release in 1983 for television and is now available from the original independent filmmaker himself, Michael Mileham; contact Michael at PO Box 1388, Idyllwild, CA 92549; or contact him at DigiFilmA@aol.com;
Michael also now has his own web page at http://members.aol.com/digifilma/mileham.html.)

produced/directed by Michael Mileham, distributed by Film Sprout (1995), 43 mins

———

THE SECRET POLICEMAN'S PRIVATE PARTS (1984)

(a compilation of comedy and music taken from the four Amnesty International benefits in 1976, 1977, 1979 and 1981. Starring John Cleese, Michael Palin, Terry Jones, Graham Chapman, Terry Gilliam, Carol Cleveland, Neil Innes and Connie Booth)

- distributed by Miramax Films/Media Home Entertainment, M295, 77 mins

———

IRON MAIDEN: FROM THERE TO ETERNITY (1992)

(a collection of 21 Iron Maiden music videos, including Can I Play With Madness *featuring Graham Chapman as an overly strict school master who has hallucinations)*

- Sony Music Video (SMV) Enterprises, 19V-49132 (ISBN 1-56406-132-9), 95 mins

———

THE SECRET POLICEMAN'S EARLY BITS (1993)

(the first comedy shows dedicated to Amnesty International, A Poke In the Eye with a Sharp Stick *(1976) at Her Majesty's Theatre and* Mermaid Frolics *(1977) at The Mermaid Theatre; Terry Jones was stage director for the second stage show)*

- Amnesty International, distributed by Columbia Tristar Home Video/Sony Music Operations (UK) CVR 21432, 78 mins

———

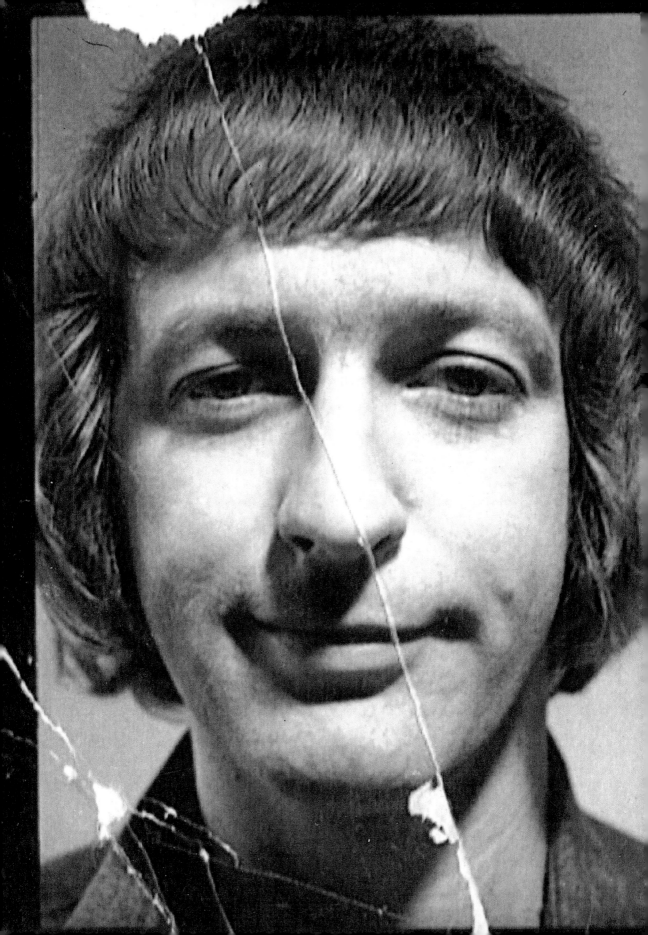

ABOUT THE GRAHAM CHAPMAN ARCHIVES

The Graham Chapman Archives were established in
1997 by David Sherlock and Jim Yoakum. The purpose
of the Archives is to preserve, protect and make
available the work of the late Graham Chapman. We
are constantly on the lookout for rare photos, videos,
films, audio recordings, scripts, newsclippings and other
artifacts by, about and/or belonging to Graham
Chapman. If you think you may have something rare
and/or unusual, and would like to donate it to the
Archives, please feel free to contact us at:
thearchives@yahoo.com

Visit us on the Web: www.gcarchives.com